Hydraulic Management in Manipur

Hydraulic Management in Manipur

Dr. Heisnam Nilkant Singh

CENTRE FOR MANIPUR STUDIES
MANIPUR UNIVERSITY
AND
AKANSHA PUBLISHING HOUSE
NEW DELHI • GUWAHATI • VISAKHAPATNAM

AKANSHA PUBLISHING HOUSE
4649-B/21, Ansari Road
Daryaganj, New Delhi-110002
Phones: 23268193, 09435116718
Email: ektabooks@yahoo.com
visit us: www.akanshapublishinghouse.com

Hydraulic Management in Manipur

First Published 2011

ISBN 978-81-8370-287-4

PRINTED IN INDIA

Published by Akansha Publishing House, New Delhi-110002 and printed at Harmain Offset Press, Delhi.

Dedicated

to

My Parents

Contents

Contents

Preface

This book begins with the pre-State Meitei civilization. What it offers is not a general survey of the history of Manipur but a close study of water related works. It is time the historians particularly of this region explore some new themes in greater detail. I myself is struck of wonder to see the vast literary sources preserved by our forefathers. However, I devote to study precisely the various water work programmes carried out by the Meitei kings and their subjects from time to time.

This book highlights the nature of statecraft initiated or formulated by the Meitei kings. It also provides a great advantageous to the young researcher of this region to investigate extensively in different spheres of the Meitei kingdom. On the other hand, extensive study of different literary texts recorded about the water works encourage me to interpret the sources in objective way. I try sincerely to make the literary sources to read in scientific historical manner.

I show my gratitude to Mr.Ch.Hemchandra Khaba, Naoremthong, Imphal for providing me all the literary sources and moral encouragement. I am very thankful to Prof. K.K. Das, Department of History, Manipur University, Canchipur for his academic assistance. I thank Mr. Kh. Kulachandra Singh who took the responsibility of the computer typing of this book. I am also grateful to my wife Mrs. H. Pancharani Chanu who shared with me in every academic activities of mine.

Dr. Heisnam Nilkant Singh

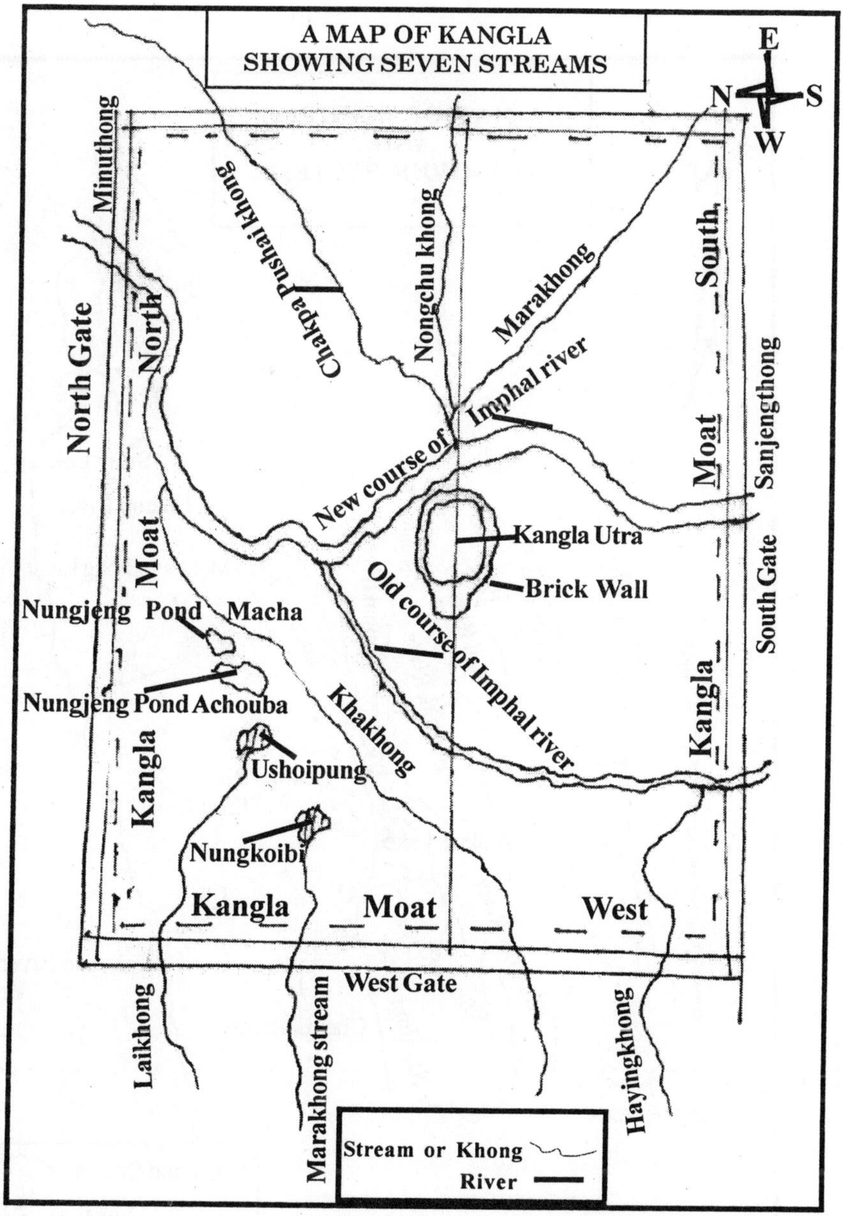
A MAP OF KANGLA
SHOWING SEVEN STREAMS
E
N
S
W
Minuthong
Chakpa Pushai khong
Nongchu khong
Marakhong
South
North Gate
North
Imphal river
New course of
Moat
Sanjengthong
Kangla Utra
Brick Wall
Moat
Old course of Imphal river
South Gate
Nungjeng Pond Macha
Nungjeng Pond Achouba
Khakhong
Kangla
Kangla
Ushoipung
Nungkoibi
Kangla Moat West
West Gate
Laikhong
Marakhong stream
Hayingkhong
Stream or Khong
River

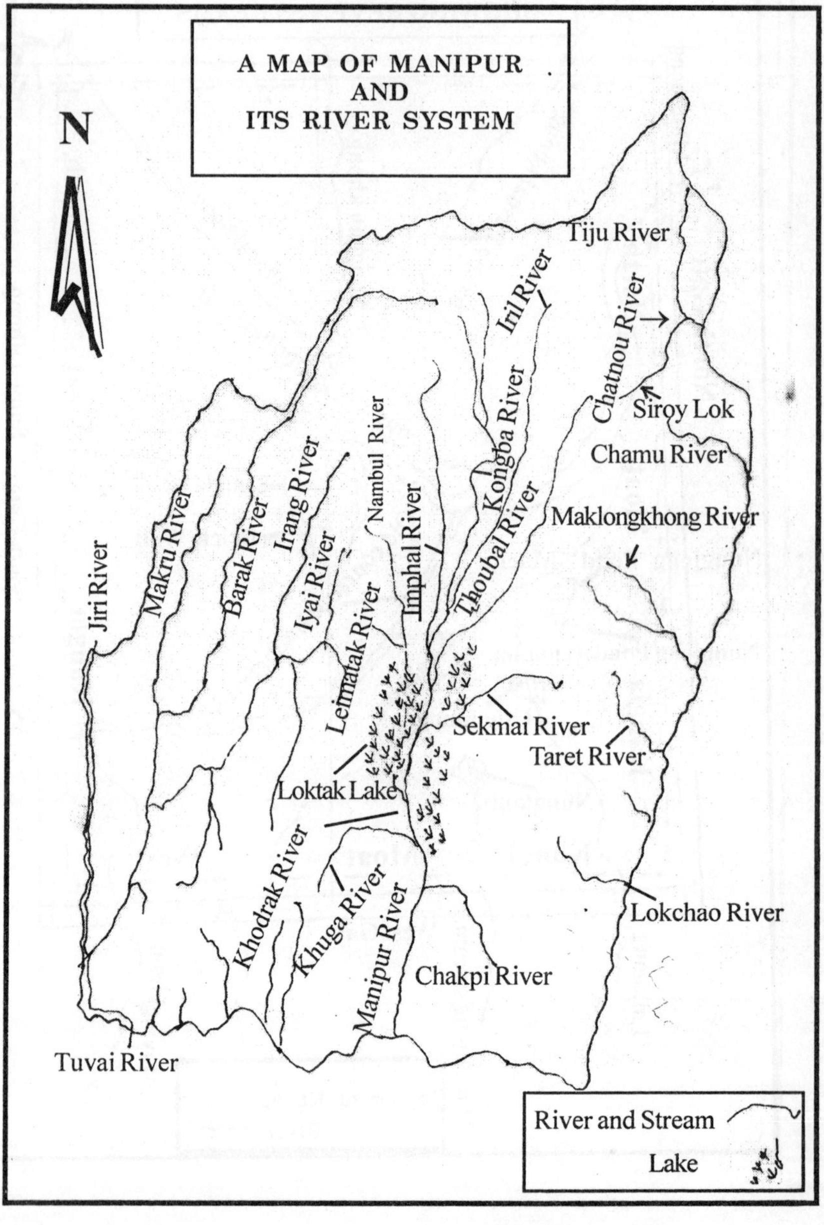
A MAP OF MANIPUR
AND
ITS RIVER SYSTEM
N
Tiju River
Iril River
Chatnou River
Siroy Lok
Chamu River
Kongba River
Nambul River
Irang River
Barak River
Makru River
Jiri River
Maklongkhong River
Imphal River
Thoubal River
Iyai River
Leimatak River
Sekmai River
Taret River
Loktak Lake
Khodrak River
Khuga River
Manipur River
Lokchao River
Chakpi River
Tuvai River
River and Stream
Lake

A MAP OF THE VALLEY OF MANIPUR AND ITS IMPORTANT RIVERS AND LAKE SYSTEM

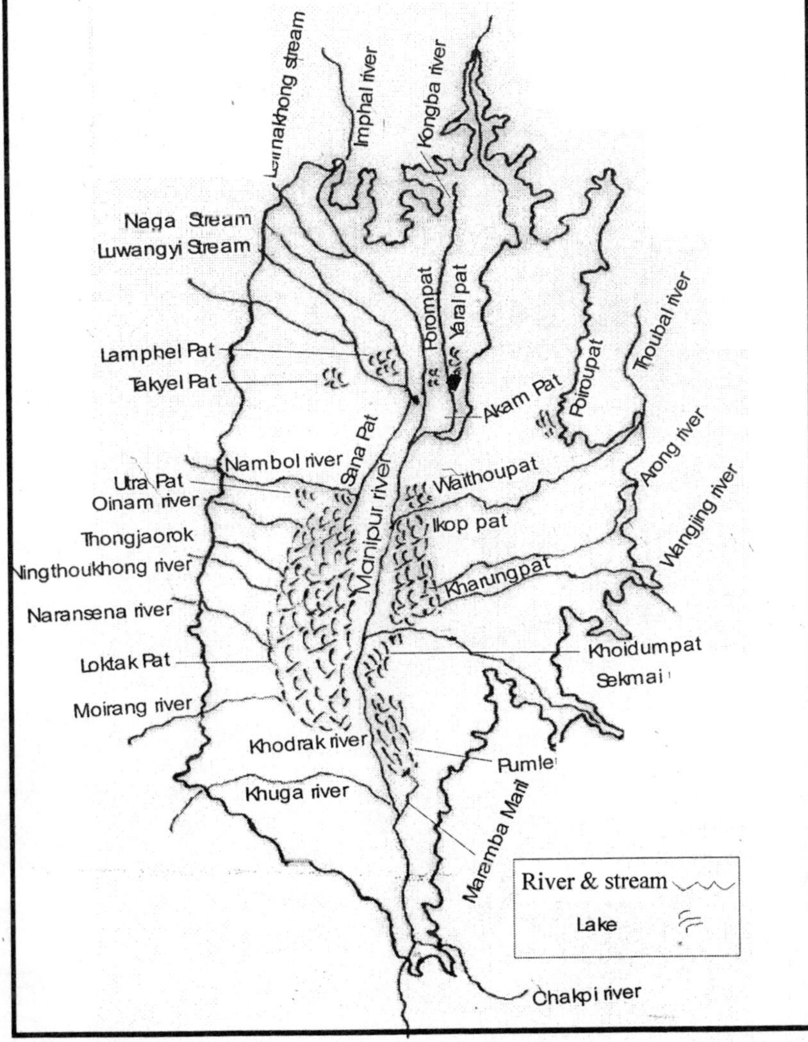

1

Land, People and Ecology

The study of hydraulic programme of the kingdom of Manipur was to focus an extraordinary power source of the State over his subjects. In fact, king generally planned a systemetic water control work to bring the entire population under his iron hand. His main perspective was ever to establish his despotic strength. From the dawn of the Meitei, civilization till the first half of the 20th century, water management works were successively carried on by the State authority to make enlighten his despotic power. Therefore, king systematised water, related institutions and posts including *Lallup* service (labour institution), *Urunghanba* (forester), *Hiruhanba* (Supervisor of boat), *Shoysenba* (Supervisor of fishing weir) and *Phunanshellungba* (Supervisor of land).

The State acquired the necessary labour from the *lallup* institution in time for hydraulic works. *Urunghanba* was usually assigned to clear the bush of the river banks and he was responsible to cut down the falling trees on the rivers. During the rainy season, violent river flood carried all the loose trees grew at the river banks and caused to fill up the river. The normal flow of river current was frequently disturbed. *Urunghanba* was liable to take up precutionary measure for clearing all the big and small trees scattered or deposited to the river beds. Considerably, his work was treated as a part of repairing river bank and draining river beds. Hiruhanba was responsible to make transport and fishing boat. King deputed *Shoysenba* to look after royal fishing shoys or weir to collect fish. *Phunanshellungba* took care of distributing cultivable land and collected tax.

However, the four *panas* were responsible to organise ten men each and formed Forty *Pallungba Maroi* (a group of forty workers). Out of these forty workers, 10 *Pallungba Maroi* (a group of ten workers) were assigned to look after *Ething Panthing* (block of water by raising dikes), *Ethei Loukhong* (management of irrigated canal), *Lambel-Thong* (road-bridge) and *Keiroi-Hiten* (Keiroi - collector of paddy and *Hiten* river bank). They carefully viewed the river banks settle by the Keiroi groups.[1]

The present inquiry penetrates hydrological knowledge possessed by the Meitei kings. By using premitive non-mechanised method, they undertook successfully to dig canals, river banks and ponds, to raise dikes, to repair river beds and to make *shoy* (weir). Historical and literary records obviously specify the way how to dig river beds. During the winter or dry season, the river current was blocked by making dikes and then the lower portion of the river was normally excavated.

The hydraulic culture is comprised of some fundamental mechanisms such as king or leader, labour, rain or climate, topographical structures and water sheds. The hydromanagerial behaviour of a kingdom is largely determined by both rainfall regime and climate of the region. Probably, the management and distribution of pattern of water are highly influenced by the natural physiography factors including topographical features, geological formations and types of vegetation. These factors may modify the climate and frequency of rainfall.

As the society developed in Manipur, simple or loose water management regime came to exist. However, with the gradual establishment of political society, a complex form of water management flourished. Since the early period, the idea of hydromanageral work was speculated upon by several personalities or clan chiefs.

Generally hydraulic work is considered as a cyclic work. Having got manipulation of landscape or topography of a particular region or kingdom, the system itself is successfully operated by the authority. On the other hand, water is absolutely required for sustaining life and it is of great importance to be used as a means of political tool in order to maintain power. The traditional Meitei villagers also had strong sense of water control. An obvious example is the storage of water behind smaller dikes or dams built across the stream in order to supply necessary water to their agricultural fields. Various water supply systems that obtained their water from rivers or streams could be recycled several times before it finally joined main river or lakes. Both the villagers and the State authority (kingdom of Manipur) displayed consummate skill in collecting, storing and distributing surface run of water or water of water bodies for their needs, and in devising means of protection against floods although often these measures remain inadequate.

Different scholars such as Karl A Wittfogel, E. Hunt, R.C. Hunt, Henery J.M. Claessen, Steward etc. have their views regarding hydraulic hypothesis either as a process of State formation or as means of the management of the State. Wittfogel's original hypothesis that large-scale irrigation work, efficient organization and effective management are primarily necessitated for a hydraulic State. However, once such hydraulic system is set forth, hydraulic economy characterized by division of labour, intensive cultivation and co-operation on a large scale inevitably developed. After him modified versions regarding of water works and power of the State are being revived.[2]

Barbara Price clearly states the relationships between social and technological systems that concern of water control. She makes two separate statements. One is the cause and effect relationship between irrigation and various parts of the socio-cultural relationship.[3] Claessen believes that irrigation serves to intensify or help in the development of centralization of State power.[4] E. Hunt convincingly mentions that there is no simple relation between despotism and irrigation but there is a clear relation between water control and the sources of power of the ruling elites of the irrigated society.[5]

The early Meitei civilization was geographically isolated from expanding culture centres till the 18th century A.D. The kingdom had number of administrative units like *Pana* (district), village etc. It had also various bureaucracies or functionaries which reached down to the districts and village levels. In addition to this, there were workers directly concerned with the administration and management of water sources and points. The water-works of which Manipur was a part had been centrally organized and developed since the dawn of pre-State period. It was continued even after the State formation as indispensable task.

Probably, the State took the entire responsibility for planning, construction, management and organization of a series of water-works. The Meitei kings extensively exercised their power over different decision-making and also over the management works. Though the king was at the top of the political strata, different aspects of water control were envisaged to lower levels of administrators like the bureaucrates and district and village functionaries which were existed within the State. In this regard, the degree of centralization of the Meitei king could be properly measured by a particular water control programme. The Meitei kings timely organized necessary labour, developed military defence of water points and performed rituals to handle easily the watersheds and water points. These practices involved money, power and specialized role which could not be met by an ordinary power but by the king or political leader alone. Thus, the variable water controlling programmes certainly provide a better chance to the Meitei kings to centralize his power. The centralized tendency was intensified when the field irrigation was inaugurated by king Garibaniwaz.

Since the hydromanagerial system was prevelent in early Meitei society, the kingdom possessed networks to control of the physical environment i.e. amount of water available and man-made dams, dikes, canals, weirs etc. On the other hand, all the water-control mechanisms within a Meitei social structure were the handyworks of managers and his associates. However, social groups political institutions, decision-makers or political leaders and water management plan are in the same line. While in this situation, the Meitei kings were supreme in all matters. Gigantic river dredging works, repairing of embankment of river, construction of canal and irrigated canal, tank, diversion of river course, making dikes and weirs and creation of defensive moats were carried out under the complete order of the king. When the dispute arose over the supplies and distribution of water, he intervened and resolved the dispute. Many villagers had their autonomous water irrigated management system. It was established by manipulating streams and by making communal canals. Whenever srious dispute cropped up over the water distribution among themselves the king resolved the matter. The King's presence in all the rituals of water-works relating to commission and inauguration to safe and control all the water points could establish legitimate right over the social environment. The connection between socio-political and religious functions of water-works and the Meitei king caused to develop highly centralized power.

Physically Manipur is divided into three parts: (a) hilly region, (b) lake region and (c) river valley regions. The hills are the sources of the rivers and valley was formed by the sediments brought down by the rivers. The Imphal valley is about 700 sq. kilometres surrounded by the hill ranges. Besides, there are smaller valley strips in the western and eastern slopes of the State. The central valley of Manipur occupies only nine per cent i.e. 1843 sq.km of its total geographical area i.e. 22,327 sq. km.[6] There are number of lakes in different places of the valley. Loktak is one of the biggest fresh water lake comprising about 200/400 sq.km. (The area of the lake is extended during the rainy season). A number of streams and rivers of north and west fall into Loktak lake from which emerges river named Khodrak.

In the valley there are smaller hill ranges running in different directions. The valley itself at an elevation of 790 metres about the Mean Sea level. The general shape of the valley is an irrigular oval.[7] Its length is about 85 km and the breadth is about 35 km. The highest ground of the valley is towards the north, the capital area. The lowest is at the Loktak and its adjoining areas, towards the south and southwest, the ground again rises. The general conformation of the valley is that of a shallow saucer.

Generally the rivers of Manipur can be classified into two drainage systems like Chindwin-Irrawaddy system and Ganga-Brahmaputra system. The rivers draining into the Chindwin-Irrawaddy system comprise Imphal river and its tributaries which run only in the valley area whereas the river runs itself into the Ganga-Brahmaputra system. Barak and its tributaries drain the hill region of Manipur and pass into the Bangladesh territory.

Imphal river rises from Bolenpat of Senapati district. It flows from north to south. The important tributaries of Imphal river or Manipur river are Iril, Sekmai, Khodrak, Kongba, Thoubal, Kakching or Sekmai, Maramba Marin canal. Iril river originates from north-east of Mao and it joins to Imphal river at Lilong. Awang Sekmai river rises from Koubru range and it connects to Imphal river at Khonghampat. Khodrak river derives from Loktak lake and it falls into Imphal river at Khodrak Echin. Kongba river merges from Kongba Maru and it unites with Imphal river at Kongba Meilombi. Thoubal flows from Huimi hill of Ukhrul District and it finally merges into Imphal river at Irong of Mayang Imphal Chakpi river arises from southern hills of Chandel District and it meets Imphal river at Serou. Sekmai or Kakching river descends from southern hills and it mingles with Imphal river at Sekmaijin. Finally, Imphal or Manipur river joins Chindwin river of Myanmar. Nambul river rises from Kangchup and it merges into Loktak Lake. The important tributaries of it are the Naga stream and the Nambol river. Moirang river arises from Thangjing Maru and it falls into Loktak lake. Heirok or Wangjing river comes down from Heirok range and joins to Ikop lake. Arong river rises from Ingourok area, runs across from east to west, and finally meets Ikop lake.

Barak, the longest and largest river of Manipur rising from the northern ranges of Senapati, drains the western half of Manipur State. It flows a south westernly course. The important tributaries of the Barak river are the Makru, the Irang, the Leimatak, the Maklang, the Jiri, the Tepai. The Makru river rises from Makru or Barail range of Tamenglong and it flows into Barak river. No part of the course of Makru is navigable.

Varieties of fishes are well stocked in this river. Irang river originates from north of Yang Pugilong ranges at the west of Karong. It runs across narrow and deep gorges. It joins Barak river near Tipaimukh. Both, Leimatak and Ijei rivers which rise from the western slopes of Laimaton ranges are the two important tributaries of Irang river. Besides, Irang receives other smaller mountain streams, before it falls into Barak river.

Tepai river running from Mizoram flows to Barak at Tipaimukh. Jiri river forms the boundary between Manipur and Assam. It arises in the hills to the north-east of Cachar District and runs across nearly south Godam Ghat then turns to west until it meets the Jiri Ghat from where it moves to south again and after about a course of 12 miles it joins the Barak river. Then Barak river traverses Cachar valley and Sylhet plain. Finally it meets the mighty Brahmaputra river in Bangladesh.[8]

Apart from these two major river system, there are number of smaller eastward running rivers near Indo-Myanmar border region. These run into eastern hilly track of the Manipur State. The important river among them is Yu which falls into Chindwin river of Myanmar. Some of the important tributaries are the Taret, the Tuyangbi, the Lockchao, the Lalim Lok, the Thuidam etc. These arise from the eastern ranges of Manipur. Both Chingai and Chamu rivers flow over the northern part of Ukhrul District in Manipur and merge with the Chindwin river.[9]

'Patki Hourakpham' (Source of Lake) an ancient literary text records as many as 42 lakes. These are given below:

> *"Chakha Pat, Hyeng Pat, Lampun Pat, Waishel Pat, Luwangyi Pat, Yangkoi Pat, Kokcha Pat, Thangching Pat, Serikok Pat, Khakoktao Pat, Nungchengpat, Yilil Pat, Langyam Pat, Kakwa Pat, Chingak Pat, Lilrong Pat, Thoupal Pat, Teltha Pat, Yikok Pat, Haiyen Pat, Khaopakhong Pat, Wuchiwa Pat, Laikol Pat, Thamlal Pat, Phumlou Pat, Khaka Pat, Leimatak Pat, Chingmahut Pat, Yimuyilal Pat, Laikhom Pat, Leisom Hilel Pat, Kailakhong Pat, Wunungta Pat, Takhel Pat, Wulikhong Pat, Kontha Pat, Ngaching Pat, Polapi Pat, Laicha Pat, Thaku Pat and Kekrupat."*[10]

In addition to these lakes, there were number of lakes like *Akampat, Hichamyaichampat, Lamphel Pat, Leicheng Pat, Uphongpat, Porompat, Keishampat, Yaral Pat, Uchekon Pat, Mantak Pat, Poirou Pat, Waithou Pat, Kharung Pat, Ngangou Pat.* Many of these afore-mentioned lakes have become extinct. However, Loktak and Pumlen lakes still exist.

Naturally, these lakes played a great role in monitoring the climate of the kingdom and in providing livelihood materials as well as transport facility to the people. Naturally, the ecological environment developed a habitate which attracted people/communities to live in the watershed system of the kingdom. From time to time, the people inhabiting the lakes and its surrounding areas were able to develop different mechanisms mould and sustain the lake environment. They would gather various edible aquatic and non-aquatic plants from the lakes. They caught fishes by using traps, spiked spears and nets. Of course, the demographic structure changed due to increase of community population and immigrant ethnic groups. This ever changing trends of population brought to manage even the marshy areas of the lake for their expansion of habitation. The people of Moirang and Kanglei practically established settlement mounds in the marshy and swampy areas and even the lake banks. By diverting river course and making canal and filling day by day, the lakes were transformed into habitational areas and cultivable fields. Nambul was once the most important source of water which drained itself in the Uphongpat lake. When the Nambul river was diverted eastward by cutting new canal, this lake came to dry up due to the absence of riverine water supply. During the reign of Nara Singh lake like Thiyam pat were transformed into cultivable fields. The lakes such as Keishampat, Hichamyaichampat, Porompat, Akampat, Lamphelpat etc. dried up by draining water through canals, enchroachment of human settlement and siltation. Likewise other lakes scattered around the valley came to disappear one by one. The water of Pumlenpat lake was also monitored by draining of water through Maramba Marin canal which was connected to Imphal river. Such a canal largely brought an advantage a control of river flood by catching excess water during the rainy season and it also enabled the supply of water to the river during the dry season.

Obviousely, different rivers like the Imphal, the Iril, the Kongba, the Naga, the Thoubal which flowed across the valley provided suitable environment for the prestine Meitei civilization. The rivers are significant factors to make the valley ferfile and supply usuable water to provide easy means of communication to the earliest forms of transport. The rivers were managed and controlled by the Meitei kings and their associates to adjust and adapt to the existing environment. The successful water management and several kinds of devices became the life source to the early Meitei civilization and these equipped the governance of the kingdom peacefully.

Generally, the climate of Manipur varies according to her topographical elevation. The State is under the influence of sub-tropical monsoon climate. It's rainfall differs from 110 cm to 350 cm and the average annual rainfall is 74 inches to 100 inches. However, the season of Manipur is divided into four. These are Pre-Monsoon (March and April), Monsoon (May to September), Retreating Monsoon (October and November) and Winter (December to February). Usually, in Manipur rainfall starts from March. But the South West Monsoon reaches Manipur in the month of May and it continues up to October. The North East Monsoon known as Retreating Monsoon starts from the last part of October. Thus, the success and failure of crops of the State entirely depended on Monsoon rain. It also highly influenced upon the occupational activities of the peoples inhabiting both the highland and the valley regions.[11] According to E.W. Dun:

> "the climate at once rainy and temperate cover the hills in the western portion with thick forests and induces the inhabitants to grow rice, causes numerous rivers, streams and marshes, and encourage aquatic and water loving plants. Forests in the east was not thick as in the west. Oak replaced bamboo, firs for Nageshwar, drier climate

produced a lighter and different kind of jungle. The villages in the valley were situated on the banks of the rivers or edge of the lakes so that every household had some water near it."[12]

According to R.D.Oldham:

"the succession of beds of Manipur is of Cretaceous rocks, accompanied by Serpentine rocks which are younger than Cretaceous rocks and the associated sendimentary rocks."[13]

These rocks belong to Disang and Barail series. Barail series spreads in many parts of Assam, Nagaland, and Manipur. Disang series is almost consentrated in north-eastern part of Ukhrul District and south-eastern part of Chandel District of Manipur and Barail series covers a considerable north-western tracts of Senapati, the south-western part of Tamenglong and Churachandpur districts of Manipur.[14]

Between these two rock series, the central valley of Manipur with a lake of thick alluvium deposit is situated. E.W. Dun writes that:

"the formation of the central plain of Imphal was due to stream being blocked by some convulsion of nature."

However, some geologists believe that the valley was formed as a result of lake filled up by river borne sediments. Once upon a time, water occupied whole of the present central upliftment in the southern mountain which brought to make a reversal drainage system through which water occupying the valley area got drained out.[15]

With the discovery of some prehistoric sites in the surrounding hill areas of Manipur. O. Kumar Singh an Anthropologist maintains that Manipur for the first time got enlisted in the prehistoric map of the world. It profoundly influenced on the social scientists of Manipur to reconstruct a scientific history of Manipur. It pushed back the history of Manipur from early Christian era to c.4000 B.C. Archaeological study deals with man and his relation with the environment and his recorded achievements. Prehistory is the period of man's existence since he emerged from his animal ancestry. The Archaeologists reconstruct the history of this period through the study of stone artifacts, bone tools, potteries, plants, animal fossils etc. left by them. Historians have classified the man's past into three periods like prehistory, protohistory and history. In short, the written records alone cannot be sufficient to give a complete picture of protohistorical and historical period, so archaeological findings are used to supplement them. Archaeological research of prehistory in Manipur is very recent and is still not fully developed. But the explored evidence of prehistoric sites show the prevelance of Palaeolithic, Haobinhian and Neolithic culture in Manipur. The important caves and shelters sites in the hills of Manipur which provided shelters to the prehistoric men are Songbu cave of Chandel district (4000 B.C.), Khangkhui cave (3000 B.C.) and Hundung of Ukhrul district, Tharon cave of Tamenglong district, open air sites at Machi of Chandel district, Nongpok Keithelmanbi of Senapati district, Napachik at Wangu of Bishnupur district, Panjao Pallumching at Kakching of Thoubal district and Phunanching of Imphal East district.[16]

According to archaeologists, the excavated sites of the stone age is divided into three stages such as

1) Paleaolithic culture,

2) Haobinhian culture and

3) Neolithic culture.

Palaeolithic Culture

Palaeolithic tools discovered from Machi a Maring village of Chandel District are chopper and chopper-chopping. Tool types found in Khagkhui cave, a Tangkhul village of Ukhrul district are chopper, scraper, cleaver, burin, blade, flake, bone tools and funeral remains. Tools like chopper, scraper, notch, graver, blade, flake and split pebbles are explored from Nongpok Keithelmanbi of Senapati District. At Songbu cave site of Chandel District, some tools i.e. handaxe, chopper, scraper point and flakes are also found. The cultures of Khangkhui cave, Machi cave and Nongpok Keithelmanbi can be compared with the Late Choukoutien Culture of China whereas Songbu cave culture will be closely associated with the South East Asian Choukoutien Culture. Between 30000 to 10000 B.C., the Choukoutien man and Pre-Australoid man were spreading throughout the South East Asian regions.[17] Some of the late Choukoutien man would be inhabiting to these Palaeolithic sites of Manipur. As stated above, the first habitation in Manipur would start in hill areas.

Haobinhian Culture

However, Haobinhian culture is a cultural pattern based on the tools found of Haobini village of North Vietnam. In Manipur Haohinhian tools were unearthed from different sites of Tharon cave and Nongpok Keithelmanbi. The tools explored from these areas are edged ground pebble tool, cleaver, scraper, pointed edged-ground pebble tool, ground stone tool, proto-handex etc. It is believed that this cultural period will be from *c.*12000 B.C. to *c.*5000 B.C. It spreads in many areas of South East Asia like Thailand, Burma, Malyasia, Vietnam and Manipur. Around the c.12000 B.C. Haobinhian people entered Manipur and settled at Tharon. But these people would establish their habitational area at Nongpok Keithelmanbi between c.6000 B.C and c.5000 B.C.[18]

Neolithic Culture

Both Palaeolithic and Hoabinhian people of Manipur lived in the hill areas while the Neolithic cultural people used to settle on hill and in plain areas. The important archaeological exploration sites of Neolithic age of Manipur are Nongpok Keithelmanbi, Phunan and Napachik. Many cultural remains that were discovered are chisel, hoeblade, traingular axe, plain and corded ware, tripod ware, Phunan or geometric design decorated ware. The date of this culture will be around 3500 to 500 B.C. South East Asia Neolithic culture commenced from 6000 B.C. years ago and these cultural people were moving throughout this region. But in Manipur, different neolithic hoards begun to enter around 3500 B.C. and it continued for several years.[19] More or less, "Manipur valley was already inhabited by the neolithic men in or around 2000 B.C. Hoabinhian cultural traits point to the Austroloid who migrated to Manipur before the advent of the Tibeto-Burman Mongoloid who followed them around 1000 B.C. In different successive period various hoards of people entered in Manipur through hill routes. On many occasions different people went through the valley of Manipur. Before 900 B.C., one Saka prince Aviraj entered the hill route of Manipur. He crossed the valley of Manipur and reached to Ava through South Eastern hill route of Manipur. His passage exemplifies that the hill route of Manipur was actively used since the prehistoric time. Those of the hill routes used by the people are given below:

(a)

"1. Heirok hill range route connected to Kabow valley/Shan, Ava, China and other South Eastern countries.
2. Aimol hill range route connected to Kabow valley/Shan, Ava,China and other South Eastern countries.
3. Ngarachingjin hill range route connected to Kabow valley/Shan, Ava, China and other South Eastern countries.
4. Maring hill range route connected to Kabow valley/Shan, Ava, China and other South Eastern countries.

(b)

1. Tongjeimaril hill route connected to Cachar, Takhel,Tripura and Western countries.
2. Khonjai hill route connected to Cachar, Takhel,Tripura and Western countries.
3. Akui hill route connected to Cachar, Takhel,Tripura and Western countries.

(c)

1. Chingkhei Haram (north-east) hill route connected Tekhao (Assam) and other Western Countries."[20]

A large number of megaliths both stone and wooden monuments are erected by different hill tribes of Manipur. These remains of the Megalithic culture are still a living tradition among the hill tribes. Since the early time, the hill tribes such as Mao, Maram, Zemi, Liangmei, Tangkhul, Maring and Anal and others raised stone megaliths.[21] Generally, these have their legends of origination from the caves found in the hill areas. These sources of information practically highlight the human habitation in the hill areas since prehistoric period. These are quite similar to those erected by the tribals of the Andaman and Nicobar islands. South Indian traits are also visible at times.

Lai Khunda a literay text of the Meiteis substantially tells about the establishment of settlement on the hillocks and higher or elevated places of the central part and peripheral regions of the valley during the pre-Pakhangba and his times. "Cheklei Phanba occupied Enathai area. Nongbal Leirelchamba lived in Chingmai. Luwang Punshiba dwelt in Shoirel Eemaru (Luwang Makubi area - present Kangchup area). Luwang Selhongba also set up a habitational area at Kouba Napachik (present Langol hill area). Probably Luwang Koi Manao inhabited to Thok Kachin (Langol Thongak Chingjil) Pamang Heirinba settled on Khonghampat. Nongbasu Taba who was descendant of Luwang lived in Kaklou Touthang (present Touthong village). Langjing Phela was found to dwell by Thaba Melei. Phetup Phidai Chanu resided at Thangkhu Thanglel. Chikai Pangkoiba make a habitational abode at Kangpokpi (present Imphal municipality area). Nongmainu Yaoreibee Kakla Lamcheng settled on Leipung Chara. Tanthong Lokpaiba lived in Phouwa Ching (Loijing Phouwoibi Ching or hill) Pachi Chukok and others created dwelling place at Loihaba Phuba Ching (hill area of Phubala - this area should be the west of the present Phubala village). Pasi Kangba Khawangba lived in Haoman Ikai area (territory of Ithai Keiremba). Khwa Ningthou or chief dwelt in Loiya Kangbung (Kamong area). Leima Haoreima Ningthou Panthang Soinaibi resided at Khura Haora Lamangdong (present Bishnupur). Kuki Ahong (another name of Thongarel) was very courageous to set up good settlement area at Waikok Lamhal (somewhere of Nongmaijing hill area). Lairen Khamtoubi Khamtouba used to live in Chinga Loukhong.

Jommaibi Jomaiba resided on Chinga and Pishum hillocks respectively. Laiki Achouba better known as Thongarel initiated to create habitational site at Waikok Lamhal area. These aforesaid areas were possibly installed in the west of the valley of Manipur.

Further, the text mentions more habitational areas set up by the different personalities. Heirem Loinai was responsible to create a settlement place at Kontha Saban (present Kontha area of Heingang constituency). Akong Tattaba Arai Kangdaba (a group of people frequently appeared in that region where they were going to make a habitational area) inhabited to Khomidok Ungam Phaibu area. Haorong or Haorok people used to reside at Chingnangkhu Chengnunglen area. Khaba Phandongba, a chief of Khaba clan, settled on Tongjeng Phaiphek site. Moriya Phambalcha occupied Teban Heirem Khok Kumma Naosang created a settlement site at Longmai Khunkhu area. Keirao Chinabok area was made settlement site by Taliya Likhun Tola. Phunan Telheiba Koijing Koimanao descendant of Luwang took a great responsible to set up a habitational place at Withou Khamput Thongraobee and Toknakha Takna areas. No doubt, these settlement sites were mainly formed in the east of the valley.[22]

Scholars believe that possibly around 2000 B.C. pre-historic man came down to the valley and they settled in valley areas. As many as seven layers of neolithic sites of Napachik were excavated. Out of thse, the fourth layer has been dated *c.*1450 B.C. The first layer could be between 500 B.C. to 200 B.C. According to T.C.Sharma the late neolithic age of north east India is *c.*200 B.C.[23] King Kangba was the first Chenglei king born at Koubru hill and he was succeeded by his son Maliya Phambalcha who got married to Chakpa girl.[24] The above evidence indicates that the Chakpa ethnic group lived somewhere on the valley or peripheral foot hills who were contemporary to the Chengleis of Koubru. During the pre-Pakhangba period, Maliya Phambalcha was supposed to rule in 1397 B.C.[25] As a matter of fact, the Chengleis of Koubru range would be the contemporary of fourth layer of Napachik Neolithic site. Some of the hill ranges like Koubru, Laimaton, Thangjing, Marjing, Nongmaiching etc. were frequently connected to the folk tales and literary works about the origin of the proto-Meiteis. As stated above, Thangjing range is the mythological and historical place for the origin of the Moirangs. It is also referred in the tales and literary texts that Koubru range is also the first home place of seven salais or clans. The above sentence is made more convenient by Meitei proverb i.e. "*Awang Koubru Asuppa, Leimalei khunda Ahanba Salalik Mapal Thaba, Nongthrei Mapan Lingba*"[26] (Supreme Koubru range is the first settlement site, so important and unparallel). Naothingkhong Phambal Kaba ancient literary text records that Shelloi-Langmai tribes at first lived on the Nongmaiching hill and they performed jhuming cultivation in the hill areas.[27] It is supported by a statement given by W.McCulloch that "in pristine times the Moirang tribes came from the south, the direction of the Kookies, the Koomal from the south, the direction of the Murrings and the Looang from the North west, the direction of the Koupoees." The descendents of these tribes used to settle respectively in different places of the valley in different periods. He believed that this present Manipuri language was the genesis of the unification of the different tribes under the name of the Meiteis. It has very close similarity to the languages spoken by these tribes. He further emphasises that during the coronation ceremony of the Meitei king, the use of Naga dresses both by Raja and Ranee and the *Yim-Chao* (big house), the royal residence of the Meitei king was made in Naga fashion. It became customary. Similarities of the preservation of some common customs, their superstitions preserved in relics and the stories of their ancestors have proved the close relationship between the Meiteis and the Nagas themselves. An apparent closeness of the original groups between the Meiteis and the Nagas cannot be ruled out.[28]

B. Kulchandra Sharma develops a long history of migration and settlement of different ethnic groups in Manipur. His works are mainly based on literary, tales, archaeological findings and contemporary historical writings. Some of the ethnic groups like

Chenglei, Khaba Nganba, Nongban, Nongyai migrated to Manipur from the east following the upstream of Manipuri rivers and settled on Koubru hill ranges. Another Himalayan and Tibeto-Burman admixture tribe like Kabui and Maomei migrated to Koubru hill ranges of Manipur from west. Chakpas, a branch of Tibeto-Burman speakers who had cultural similarities with the Pyu of Burma entered in Manipur from east following the course of the Manipur river. They scatterly settled on the upper valleys of Kongba, Iril and Imphal rivers. They mainly concentrated in Sekta, Sekmai, Andro areas etc. Another Chin ethnic immigrants are the Kharam, the Khende, the Mande, the Chairel etc. They entered in Manipur from Chin hill region of Myanmar. They used to inhabit the south-western region of Manipur.[29]

Different scholars highlight that during the proto-historic period, Tai-Lai or Lai ethnic groups were inhabiting to Manipur. When they came in Manipur, they accompanied with the Wangam ethnic group. Besides, different hords of Tai ethnic group entered in Manipur during this period.

In general most of the social scientists in Manipur unanimously resolved that since the dawn of proto-history till the 18th century, the cradle of the Shan or Tai group are the direct north-eastern neighbour of the ancient Meitei kingdom. According Prof. Chen Lufan, "the home of the ancient Shan people was not far from the Central Yunnan Plateau and the Shan people originated from the Homo Orientalist,"[30] He further describes that the wide arc-shaped land mass stretching from the west of the Red river to the upper reaches of the Irrawady river reaching as far as Manipur of India is the territory of the ancient Shan people.[31] Professor Fang Guoyu also states that the Shan race settled on the wide arc-shaped region extending from the west of the Red river to the upper reaches of the Irrawaddy river reaching as far as Manipur in India that is the region covering what is now Laos, Northern Thailand, the Shan State of Burma, the Assam State of India and also the South-Western part of Yunnan. He further says that since the mankind appears in this region, certainly the Shans settled on this region.

Of course, their settlement expanded and developed. The careful examination of the discovered cultural relics in Thailand. Lishuangbam and other places in 1960s proves the truth of his statement.[32]

Chen Lufan develops his theory after detailed discussion of the unearthed series of fossils of Homo Sapiens in central part of Yunnan. Those discovered fossils are the Kaiyuan Ramapithecus (10 million years) - Lufeng Ramapithecus (8 million years) - Hudic (butterfly). Ramapithecus (4-3 million years) - Homo Oritenalist (2.5 million years) - Yuanmou Man (1.7 million years) - Kichou man (100,000 years) - Lijiang Man (30,000 - 20,000 years). Moho Orientalist is considered upto now as the earliest man ever discovered on this earth. Besides, Homo Orientalist is the progenitor of the races in the eastern hemisphere. Then came the Yuanmou Man of 1.7 million years ago. In Yuanmou, there are many locations with artifacts of the Palaeolithic Age at different periods of time ranging from 6000,000 years as the upper limit to 30,000 years as the lower limit but also about a hundred remains of the Neolithic Period, scattered over the whole of Yunnan with distinctive characteristics have been discovered. From the immemorial time Yunnan has been a region of multi-nationalities, and the multifarious cultures.[33]

Though anyone does not set up any archaeological evidence regarding the Shan migration in Manipur during prehistoric, protohistoric and early historic periods, the tales and literary works frequently tell about their coming. Since the Shans are the direct eastern neighbour they would have contributed major portion of population to build a future Meitei nation.

"Ethnologically and linguistically the Meiteis are the Tibeto-Burman family of the southern Mongoloid with Austroloid, Aryans admixture."[34] The above sentence is supported by different successive statements advocated by scholars. Some are discussed below:

According to B.H. Hogdson, Moitay is originated out of the combined appelations of the Siamese 'Tai' and the Kochin Chinese" Moy.[35]

G.A.Grierson gives the linguistic background that the Meiteis belong to Tibeto Burman language. He further proves that the Meitei language is included in the Kuki-Chin sub-family of Tibeto-Burman linguistic group. Once again he asserts that the Meiteis had linguistic affinity with the Kachins.[36]

T.C. Hodson states that considerably the Shans (Tai) and Mon-Khmer influence on the Meiteis culturally and politically were very active.[37]

The above statements are again strengthened by the recent archaeological findings in various hill areas of Manipur that have shown the existence of Mon-Khmer speaking Austroloid, Mongoloid people in Manipur who migrated to this land before the advent of the Tibeto-Burman speakers. These Mon-Khmer elements were absorbed by later immigrants.

Mayang Kalisha belonged to Negreto-Austroloid racial admixture group who entered in Manipur in about 9th century A.D. And the Aryan elements started to migrate into Manipur from the 15th century A.D. Of course, these Western immigrants were absorbed in the Meitei population.

The cyclic discourse of Meitei civilization continued for many centuries. The civilization served as the harbour of different races. It lies between the cross-road of South East Asia and Indian sub-continent. The innovations and introductions of different administrative units and systems from time to time exemplify that the Meitei society was rather to develop in many spheres. The sense of responsibility as a ruler and commanding understanding of its natural topography of them make ever strike to the thinking process of the Meitei kings. They fairly demonstrated their wisdom to nurse the early Meitei civilization.They furnished all the systems according to the convenient of the administration. Possibly, they were gifted the art of administration. In 12th century Meitei king Meidingu Loiyumba codified the first written law of administration. In this regard, the Meiteis are regarded as the foremost among the South East Asian nations. Such circumstances could feed the kingdom in an unexorable path of cyclic track. Since they were competent in the field of administration, the civilization was possibly brought to an undergone development.

The extra indigenous martial quality make the Meiteis superior to her other neighbours. Since the firearm was not known to the people of Southern Himalayan and South East Asian regions, the primitive weapons like swords, spear, axe, arrow and bow were very important for war. However, the Meitei kings had *Thang Khumbomba* (Sword) and *Ta Khousunai* (spear) which possessed extraordinary godly power. These sword and spear were made in a stipulated time and day to be uninvincible. In addition to this, they developed the art of handling the sword, spear and arrow. The traditional advance weapon use technique which is the dominating reason of the Meiteis to the neighbouring rival could posed a successful response to all the challenges. Another deciesive factors of the Meiteis against her enemies were the use of cavalry and *Arambai* (deadly slings) which were not known to the enemies of the Meitei.

The early Meitei civilization was properly generated and sustained by imposing taxes on her subjects and collecting tributes and booties from the defeated rivals. Furthermore, the kingdom was properly maintained by launching some specific programme like proper labour organization, water management programme and effective handling of State religion to achieve the State in full-swing and to attain State apparatus.

The Meitei civilization evolved through a long historical periods. The lineage-based society was the first form of social unit on the way of State evolution. It was followed by chiefdom and clan societies respectively. Definitely, the early Meitei State was established on the basis of the socio-political systems of the clans. During the pre-State period, different clan principalities like Mangang, Luwang, Chenglei, Angom, Khuman, Moirang, Khaba-Nganba, Sarang-Leishangthem, Heirem-Khunjam, Thanga-Kangbong, etc. were ruling over the river banks and periphery foot-hill of the valley of Manipur.

During the early Christian era, in the central valley region, there was a great political tussle between the Khabas and Pakhangba's group in order capture the Kangla seat of political power. In the beginning, the Khabas defeated Nongda Lairen Pakhangba; but very soon with the assistance of Moirangs retaliated successfully. Pakhangba smashed the might of the Khabas. Therefore, many of them ran away and took asylum to the area of Puleiromba, the chief of Angom principality and to the surrounding hill areas. Probably, one Khaba Nongampa surrendered to Pakhangba. Relentlessly, Pakhangba once again confronted one colonizer named Poireiton. He was finally forced to accept the suzerainty of Pakhangba.[38]

After a strong struggle against his own kinsmen, the Khabas and Poireiton, Nongda Lairen Pakhangba ascended to the throne of Kangla with the great support from Angom chief, Puleiromba, Luwang chief Langba Langmaiba and Mangang chief, Apanba. Besides, other tribes and the leaders of the Chakpas also accepted his suzerainty. Thus, Nongda Lairen Pakhangba was crowned as the first Meitei king. However, the successful war against Poireiton and Khabas, the coordination of Puleiromba, Langba Langmaiba and Apanba and the acknowledgement of Pakhangba's supremacy by tribes and Chakpa leaders could make a high degree of subordination within his own territory and outside his kingdom. The situation caused to increase manpower i.e. militia personnel and manual labour.

The confederated Meitei State was more distinguished by the existed State society and polity. The actual social relation i.e. matrimonial relation between the ruling family of the State and clan principalities should be most advantageous factor in cementing a federal unity. To a greater extend, the confederation tended to bring a tremendous development in the structure of the social and political institutions. The newly emerged early Meitei State is strengthened by introducing administrative primary institutions and conquest. These were followed by number of socio-economic and cultural innovations and changes took place during different successive rulers.

In olden day, Manipur was named differently by her neighbouring people. To the Shans or Pongs of Upper Burma, She was known as 'Cassay' and the Burmese 'Kathe.'[39] The Cacharis named her as 'Magli' and to the Ahoms she was known as 'Makeli.'[40] The indigenous names of Manipur were Kanglei(pak), Poirei (pak) and Meitrabak.

To a greater extent, the political boundary of the Meitei kingdom was decided according to the might and power of her kings. It is for the first time during the reign of Kayamba (A.D. 1467-1501), her boundary was expanded beyond the mountain barrier of Manipur. Cheitharol Kumbaba, the royal chronicle records that during Kayamba's period the boundary of Meitei State touched Mungkong in the north east, Loijiri hills in the west, Miyotong in the south and the western portion of Shamjok in the east. So, prior to Kiyamba the State of Manipur was rather small territorilly.[41]

When Lainingthou Khagemba ruled over the kingdom, the boundary of the kingdom was extended from Gwai (Barak) in the west, to the Chindwin in the east and from Maram hills in the north to the Tui Vai river in the south.[42] Sometimes the boundary was spread three or four days journey east beyond the Ningthi river and formed eastern boundary. The plains of Cachar was also made as a part of the kingdom. In the early part of the 19th century A.D., the forest between the Doyang and Bhunsiri was formed as a boundary of the kingdoms of Manipur and Ahom.[43] Culturally and politically Manipur is closely connected with the South East Asian countries. Her natural position makes her closer to the South East Asia than South Asia.

Manipur, 23°50' N latitude to 25°30' N latitude and 93°10'E longitude to 94°30'E longitude, is bounded by Nagaland in the north, Myanmar and Mizoram in the south, Assam in the west and Myanmar in the east.[44]

REFERENCES

1. Masin (MS), p.43.
2. Karl A.Wittfogel, *Oriental Despotism, A Comparative Study of*

Total Power, New Haven , Yale University Press, 1957, pp.22-23.

3. Barbara Price, *Prehispanic Irrigation in Nuclear America*, Latin American Research Review, 6:197, pp.3-7 and R.Cohen and E.R.Service (Reproduced) to *Origin of State: The Anthropology of Political Evolution*, Philadelphia, 1978,p.68.
4. Henery J.M.Classen and Pater Skalnik, *Early State*, The Hague: Mouton. 1978, p. 62.
5. R. Cohen and E.R. Service, *op.cit.*, pp.70-71.
6. R. Brown, *Statistical Account of Manipur*, Calcutta, 1874, p. 3.
7. M.T. Laiba, *The Geography of Manipur*, Imphal, 1992, p. 88.
8. R. Brown, *op.cit.*, p. 3.
9. M.T. Laiba, *op. cit*, pp.109-110.
10. Patki Haurakpham, unpublished, pp. 1-4.
11. M.T. Laiba, *op.cit*, p. 110.
12. E.W. Dunn, *Gazetteer of Manipur*, Simla, 1886, p. 6.
13. R.D. Oldham, *Memories of the Geological Survey of India*, Vol. XIX Part 4, Calcutta, Superintendent of Government Printing, 1883, p. 32.
14. Anand Benerjee and Dayal, *Investigation of Nickel and Copper Mineralization in the Moreh area, Manipur State*, Manipur Gazette No.131-E-110,August 26,1968, Imphal Government Press, p. 23. and Sultan Ahmed Ansari, Aspects of Geography of Manipur, Delhi, 1985, p. 60.
15. E.W. Dun, *Gazetteer of Manipur*, Simla, 1886, p. 2 and S.A. Ansari, *op. cit.*, p. 61
16. N. Sanajaoba Singh (ed), *Manipur Past and Present* (The Heritage and Ordeals of Civilization). Vol.I, History, Polity and Law, New Delhi, 1986, pp. 59-61, 63 and 65
17. *Report of the Archaeology Department*, Government of Manipur 1985, p. 5 and O. Kumar Singh, *Archaeology in Manipur* (Series 1), Napachik, A Stone Age site in Manipur Valley, Imphal, 1984, p. 12.
18. B. Kulachandra Sharma, *Migration and Settlement of Manipur* (From Prehistoric Age to Historical Medieval Period, Imphal, 1997, p. 13.
19. *Ibid.*, p. 16.

20. Nandalal Sharma, *Meitrabak*, Imphal, 1960, pp. 29 & 31.
21. Gangmumei Kabui, *op.cit.*, p. 50.
22. Lai Khunda, Unpublished, pp. 1-3.
23. Gangmumei Kabui, *op.cit.*, pp. 52-53.
24.. N. Angou Luwang (transcribe), *Kangbalon*, 1976, Imphal,p.5.
25. Wakoklol Thiren Amaiba Purel, 1975 in Ng. Kangjia, *History of Kanglei Eyek*, Imphal, 1975,p.7.
26. Hemchandra Khaba, *Laikao (Lai Shlmok)*, Imphal, 1996, p. 45.
27. Ch.Manihar Singh, *Naothingkhong Phambal Kaba*, Imphal, 1983, p. 24.
28. W. McCulloch, *An Account of the Valley of Manipore*, Calcutta, 1859, p. 4.
29. B.Kulachandra Sharma, *op.cit.*, pp. 32-37.
30. Chen Lufan, *When Came the Thai Race? An Inquiry Kunming*, 1989, p. 135.
31. *Ibid.*, p. 136.
32. *Ibid.*, pp. 134-135.
33. *Ibid.*, p. 136.
34. Gangmumei Kabui, *op.cit.*, p. 21.
35. G.A. Grierson, *Linguistic Survey of India*, Vol.1, Part I, Delhi (reprint), 1967, pp. 50 & 72.
36. G.A. Grierson, *Linguistic Survey of India*, Vol.III, Part III, Delhi reprint, 1967, p. 1.
37. T.C. Hodson, *The Meitheis*, Delhi (reprint), 1989, p. 10.
38. W. Ibohal Singh, *The History of Manipur, An Early Period*, Delhi, 1986, p. 192.
39. R.B. Pemberton, *Eastern Fronter of British India*, Guwahati, 1968, pp. 19-20.
40. N.Sanajaoba Singh (ed), *op. cit.*, p. 1.
41. L. Ibungohal Singh and N.Khelchandra Singh, *Cheitharol Kumbaba*, Imphal, 1967, p. 196.
42. Gangmumei Kabui, *op.cit.*, p. 216.
43. S.N.Pandey (ed), *Sources of History of Manipur*, New Delhi, 1986, p. 37.
44. W. McCulloch, *op. cit*, p. 1.

2

History of Hydraulic Management in Manipur

Human evolution takes place in various environments on this earth. Man adapts habitually to different environments. In space and time, different civilizations emerged in various parts of the world. Herbert Spencer has advocated the concept of universal evolution. As an evolutionalist, he was a strong believer in social Darwinism. It is to the credit of Spencer that he applied biological thought to politics and gave a new and solid support to the organic conception of the State.[1] Later on, scholars of various disciplines like anthropology, sociology and history are responsible for developing Spencer's biological concept of State by supplementing and renewing his assertions. They also interpreted minutely the different stages of society in their own way. No doubt, the modern anthropologists, sociologists and historians realise the existence of the pre-State societies and even the ancient State societies.

It was Lewis Henery Morgan (1877) who for the first time, described the idea of a definite stage of human history. In his book *Ancient Society* he explains that:

> 'more or less mankind commenced their career from the bottom of a scale and different stages through the peril of time by accumulating practical knowledge. Such stages of society can be catagorised into three main epochs such as savegery, barbarism and civilization. He further highlights an elaborate situation of subsequent developments of human civilization. His writing mainly

makes an understanding of development structure of primary State. He strongly pleads that the pristine State came *to birth out of consensus confederation of* different tribes and subsequent conquests of smaller tribes by a powerful tribe. He puts up an accurate example of that of the Iroquois confederacy, Roman nation and Grecian confederation had been installed by means of consensus-confederation, whereas the Aztec confederation was formed by means of war and conquest.'[2]

Frederick Engels in his book *Family, Private Property and the State*, explains the successive development in stages of mankind propounded by L.H. Morgan by supplementing important information of politics and economics. His idea of State formation is based on stratification theory. It is stated that:

> "the early State arose out of the conflicts or conquests brought about by the military class managed by a chief or king."[3]

In retrospect this model fits into the emergence of many civilizations with cultural and systemic socio-cultural value systems. Morton H. Fried has pleaded that:

> "early State emerged from the stratified society in an inexorable way out of purely local conditions."[4]

However, the facts are authorised for several parameters. Probably, intrinsic as well as external parameters has to be blended. The evolution of the Meitei State in Manipur typologically belongs to an early State which merged through different stages of human societies at different points of time the north eastern region of India. We know that the nature of early State is neither dependent nor based on its antiquity. In a strict sense, its typology is entirely determined by the nature of the formation. The study of the pristine Meitei State formation should be assessed from the bottom of society for clarity of the defining moments in its historical growth and also for the purpose of shifting truth from the many myths which have marred any truthful analysis.

The early Meitei literary texts and archaeological works clearly show that during the early period, the forefathers of the Meiteis had settled on the surrounding hills like the many other tribal groups. In fact it can be assessed that the proto-Meiteis had been akin to the tribals. Of course, they moved towards the central valley or Imphal in order to occupy new settlement areas. At that time, they were at least culturally possessed people.

To a greater extent, in the early pre-State Meitei society there were need to develop certain rudimentary socio-political units like family, lineage and clan. According to J.B. Bottomore:

> "family is supposed to have been evolved from primitive promiscuity through various forms of marriages to monogamy."[5]

During the early period, forefather of the *Meiteis* lived together under a single roof of a family. Marriage ties particularly were for an offspring preferably a son to continue the lineage of patriarchal proto-*Meitei* family. Absolutely, definite and serious mutual obligations were the essential parts of the family. They were normally under the common control of the father of the family. A big family comprised of grandfather, father, grandmother, mother, sons and daughters. However, number of the extended families were expanded due to the increase in family members as there were needs to be met by the family in different fields or work. Manpower was created thereof.

The lineage or *sagei* was formed according to their occupation and type of work alloted by the king or *Ningthou*. Thus, king was responsible to form new lineage. Such pattern of lineage formation continued till the 18th century A.D. According to *Khagemba Yumlep* the ancient *Meitei* literary text, *Keithellakpam* lineage was formed on account of his work of the guard of market. *Laishangbam* lineage was also named for caring of god. *Hairangkhongcham* lineage was entitled after the name *Heirangkhongphaba*. On the other hand, *Khundrakpam* lineage was named for holding of the post of *Khullakpa* head of the village.[6] In such ways, various number of lineages continued to be formed for many centuries according to their nature of works and posts.

'*Bamon Khunthok*', an account dealing with Brahmin immigrants in Manipur records the allotment of lineages by the Meitei kings. Subhi Narayan Brahmin came from Tripura to Manipur and he married a girl named Thoinu. He was given *Phurailatpam* lineage. Brahmin named Jenna who came from Nadia married a girl named Samdenbi of the Kumbi village. He was allotted *Bachchaspatimayum* lineage. One Brahmin named Krishna Charan Tiwari who came from Kanpur was allotted *Khuraitaba Kanouji-mayum* lineage. Brahmachari Vishnuram who came from Prayag married a girl named Punni. He was allotted the *Brahmachari-mayum* lineage.[7] Besides, number of the lineages were created along the aforesaid process.

During the reign of King Khagemba, number of Cachari Muslims were arrested as war captives and they were allowed to settle in Manipur. However, they were given local women in marriage and the authorities allotted them different lineage according to their occupation. As many as 31 new lineages were allotted to the war captive Muslims.[8] This policy shows that the Meitei society was tolerant towards the immigrants and an account of marriages with the local families an attempt was made to reconcile and integrate the people into the main society.

The size of the society was widened over time under the stress of certain circumstances like change of demographic structure through the absorbtion of immigrants and natural processes. The practical change of population structure primarily fostered the disorder among the descendant groups of the early pre-State society. Such new development brought to extend social boundary and essentially society was compelled to get categorised into number of lineage groups. Through the constant change in society, the mutual assistance among the individuals acted as a major role in cementing kinship lineage society. Kinship relation was regarded as the prime reason in the organisation of social life. Gangmumei Kabui pleads that:

> "Manipur valley in the historical time had a social system and lineage based political units which had ultimately emerged into principality."[9]

Thus, lineage was treated as the fundamental feature of all social institutions. *Piba* or chief became the head of the lineage and he was not allowed to claim more power beyond the ascribed power of the lineage society. Direct relation was to link between the lineage *Piba* or Chief and his fellow kinsmen. The concept of *Ningthouja* emerged gradually from this stage. Inevitably, there was no surplus production in lineage society due to lack of tools, lack of techniques of production, a little knowledge in the art of agriculture and the scarcity of cultivable areas. They principally engaged in vegeculture, cattle rearing, hunting and fishing. Their productive activities were restricted around the natural products.

In the past, the lineage people were the real believers in animism. They always thought that spirits caused harm to human beings, animals and vegetables and so they must be propitiated. Again the natural phenomenon around them reflected their change of ideological dimensions. The lineage people of pre-State society of Manipur worshipped the spirits of their respective *Sagei Apokpa* (the founder chief of lineage). They were not only real ancestors of the lineage or *Sageis* but also cultural heros and heroines. However, the lineage chief or *Sagei Piba* was also considered as a relegious head. He enjoyed the highest position in each and every socio-religious works. He facilitated to occupy a large role to protect his people.

Gradually, the historical social order of the pre-State society had been transformed in order to respond to material needs of its society. The changes of techniques in production, demography and lineage social structure effected the geo-economic condition and position of the society. These changes tended to shift from lineage society to village community wherever the need arose. The people induced such social changes for organizing themselves and the collectivity to a higher level of civilization.

Primarily a village arose out of the unision of different lineages. King also took a responsible part to form new villages. Welbert E. More states that:

> "village communities did not exist before the neolithic period which saw the invasion of agriculture and domestication of animals."[10]

The neolithic people of Manipur would have begun to set up their villages on the small hillock situated in the valley and peripherial foot hills. One of the important Neolithic village sites is Napachik, a small hillock located between the present *Ithai* and *Wangu* villages in Bishnupur District. Phunan village stands on the *Phunan* hill of Imphal District and *Nongpok Keithelmanbi* situated on a peripheral foot hill of Senapati District are also the other neolithic village sites. During the late chalcolithic age, a number of village communities spread to the various parts of Manipur valley. Archaeologists have discovered a number of chalcolithic villages like Mongjam, Panjao Pumlen Ching, Moirong etc.[11]

In Manipur, the neolithic village people practiced vegiculture in their *jhuming* fields. With the expansion of village settlement to the valley areas, they came to perform agriculture to the limited fields. Still cattle rearing, hunting, fishing were their predominent occupation. By and large, the village communities manufactured different types of commodities including food products, simple household tools for agriculture, fishing tools utensils etc. Exchange of goods were unavoidable tasks of the village communities. However, rice fields were the important lands held by the villagers. Besides, there were other secondary crops and commodities produced in communally owned grazing fields, fishing lakes and forest lands. The common language, common customs, common social structures, common culture etc. would have strengthened the closeness in bonding the people and the nature of the village.

In due course of time, the inter-lineage relation formed strong communal links and the head's or *Piba's* authority was no longer final in the affair of the village. Now, the village was put under the control of *Khullakpa* - the protector of the village or the family. Thus, the socio-economic and physical development gathered to change the status of the lineage *Piba* or head. The Meitei village acted as an intermediary political unit on the way to the early *Meitei* State formation. It also positioned itself in the socio-political hierarchical scenario, as well as clan based or lineage based groups.

F. Houtart and G. Lemercinier define:

> "the clan as the social-space structure by a system of kinship. In effect constitutes the social entity of reference with which groups and individuals identify themselves. It is also at the level of the clan that the instance of individual or collective authority is situated. It controls the principle means of production, the land settles important conflicts and directs the activities of lineage based groups. Finally, it is the clan which constitutes the endogamous entity"[12]

According to Gangmumei Kabui:

> "a clan of the Meitei was originally an ethnic group or tribe speaking a distinct language or dialect occupying a territory; having an autonomous principality under a ruler who was both a political chieftain and social head of the clan."[13]

A clan comprised of different village communities and ethnic villages. The union of different village under a powerful chief, absorbtion of different tribe to a powerful one and amalgamation between the tribes were the governing reasons of the formation of clan. Historical evidence proves the emergence of seven *salai* or clans like *Mangang, Luwang, Angom, Khuman, Moirang, Kha-Nganba and Sarang Leisangthem.*

The Mangang tribe absorbed number of smaller tribes like *Heirong, Lei-Hou* and *Ma-Hou*. It is believed that *Mangang salai* or clan emerged out of the ethnic fusion of *Poirei* and *Mangang* tribes.[14] *Kha-Nganba salai* or clan was the product of the amalgamation of the *Khaba* and *Nganba* tribes. The *Chenglei salai* or clan was the genesis of the ethnic blending of *Thangnga* and *Kangpong* tribes. The absorbtion of different ethnic tribes to powerful one was the basic reason for the birth of *Luwang salai* or clan. The *Luwangs* were consisted of many smaller tribes. The important tribes are *Hicham, Wakong* and *Salam.*

These small tribes also absorbed number of tribes such as *Heirem Khunjam*, *Chakpa*, *Chairel*, *Arong*, and *Mahou*. Later on, tribes like *Khumpham*, *Ngangchen*, *Haokap* and *Chingsang* were also absorbed in *Luwang* tribe one after another.[15]

The *Khuman salai* or clan was formed by the intermingling of different tribes such as *Khuman, Nongyai, Mon, Chin, Leinung, Pangal, Kalicha, Thangang, Mayang, Akoksha* and *Pong*.[16] The *Angom* clan came to emerge out of the amalgamation between the *Kongba* and the *Nongbal* tribes. Their association with the *Shelloy Langmais* resulted in the rise of the *Angom* as a powerful salai or clan. The *Moirang* tribe got an assemblage of *Keges, Moriyas, Ngongoi* tribes. In the later period, different ethnic tribes like *Mung-Yang, Rumphei, Akoksha* were absorbed to *Moirang* tribe and it became one of the powerful clan.[17]

It is alleged according to a myth that clans originated out of the limbs of body of *Guru*, the Lord of the Universe, in the form of dead cow which was cut off into seven pieces on the advice of *Sidaba Mapu* (Primeaval father). Tradition further states that *Kuptreng* received the neck and his clan was named as *Angom*. *Shentreng* received the portion of the eyes and his clan was entitled as *Ningthouja*. *Pammarengba* got the head portion of dead cow: his clan was called as *Luwang*. *Leishangtao* got the front legs and his clan was known as *Khuman*. *Konshouren's salai* or clan was *Moirang* due to receive on striped belly. *Ashangba* received left side of the head; his clan was entitled as *Khaba*. The portion of red heart was received by *Lumganba* and his clan was known as *Nganba*.[18]

Since the transformation of society from village community to clan, tremendous changes were recorded during this stage. However, the emergence of new powerful clans compelled to have undergone changes of the status of the chief. The chief could attain higher status through demonstration of his ability. Thus, the chief earned the pompus title like *Ningthou* (king) who was the ruler of the clan. The *Ningthou* or King took the responsibility of performing the rites and religious works. He could have to enjoy the position of highest priest as well as the social head. It is stated that: "a chiefly line is likely to become a priestly line"[19]

The clan *Ningthou* or king became the protector of his subjects. Hence his protection extended to the productive lands. Gradually, such protection was converted into theoretically ownership right. By using simple technology, almost every individual was likely to engage in the production of food for consumption. Actually the producers no longer could enjoy the complete autonomy in their production process. The clan people would have to produce marginal surplus which could enable them to pay a part of the products of the clan *Ningthou* or king.

The wide demonstration of wet rice cultivation brought the change of property owning system that unequal access to the means of production came to emerge. However, it resulted to stratifying the entire society which was categorised into producers and enjoyers. *Numit Kapa* an ancient literary work records the existence of distinct peasant community including slave and ruling class in *Mangang* clan society.[20] Thus, the entire *Mangang* clan society was stratified. Romila Thapar states that:

> "the establishment of peasant economy is the prime mover towards the State formation. Stratification is regarded as a pre-condition to the birth of the State."[21]

Fortunately, Nongda Lairen Pakhangba, the founder of the *Ningthouja* dynasty usurped the full stratified *Mangang* society. By defeating the *Khabas* and *Poireiton's* group and getting support of the *Angoms, Luwangs, Mangang* and receiving the acceptance of his suzerainty from the *Chakpas* and other tribes. Nongda Lairen Pakhangba successfully installed pristine Meitei State. It was a beginning of a new cultural and political trend which more often had not stabilized Meitei society. The coronation ceremonies reveal a lot about the segmentary State which Manipur was becoming soon after this watershed mark in History of Manipur's State formation.

Subsequently it was the process of amalgamation, absorbtion and conquest which were the factors that made the dependent population flourish in pre-State society. The historical evidence proves that number of tribes like *Lai-Hou, Ma-Hou* and *Heirong* were absorbed in the *Mangang* tribe. Similar happenings are also found in the *Moirang, Angom, Luwang, Khuman* tribes etc. Therefore, this subsequently significant process forced the weaker tribes to give up their full share as well as right to the powerful or main tribes. Of course, this led to increase in number of the dependent population who amalgamated in due course in several class. Considerably, in the status of the chief also came to change vertically under pressure and he became the master of bigger population. Thus, the selection of chief was essentially based on thorough demonstrative ability. Having consolidated his position he extended his sway over the dependent population.

Since the dawn of the society, family was ruled by father. When the family was transformed to lineage or *Sagei,* the right and duty was passed to *Piba* (head of the lineage). With the establishment of village, the *pibas* (heads of the lineages) were brought under the common control of *Khullakpa* (the head of the village). When the *salai clan* was formed, these village *Khullakpas* were put under the new chief like *Ningthou* king). The *Ningthou* or king belonged to a definite lineage and he was responsible to introduce the law of primogeniture. According to E.R. Service:

> "Since the primogeniture became an established custom or rule, the chief got the stability in power of leadership."[22]

Probably, the clan *Ningthou* in order to make secure his position, he designated the idea of super family and super clan. The house of *Meidingu* (Lord) of *Ningthouja* clan became the direct descendent of god. Thus, the long road from the position of the father, *Piba* to *Ningthou* or king definitely known as structural precondition played a vital role in the to birth of the institution of kinship.

Robert Carneiro observes that:

> "those regions in which areas are fertile land or good land should be surrounded by deserts or unproductive mountains or by the sea. When the population pressure results to increase competition and warfare in such region the weaker, or defeated or subjugated groups can not

> simply move away,as they typically do in region differentiated when very rich land is tightly circumscribed, subordinated groups became absolutely tied down in their lower-class or caste status."[23]

The valley of Manipur is surrounded by the mountain ranges and it is highly fertile drained by small rivers and the numerous lakes are scattered in different parts of its valley. Though, it is a sub-tropical monsoon valley, the climate is moderate around the year because of its natural location. Both riverine and lake facilities are common features throughout the valley. It attracted large number of people to settle here. It can be compared to a crucible in which large number of Ethnic Communities extracted and got integrated over a time frame.

It is recorded that during the pre-State period, various ethnic tribes entered and settled down on the fertile valley of Manipur in different successive periods. Probably, their aim of migration was to search a new habitable lands where abundant livelihood materials could be found. Those hoards of immigrants who entered into the valley of Manipur could be satisfied by fertile land, riverine facility and good climate.

In course of time, population grew under the stress of certain conditions like ethnic migration and natural birth. The eventual circumstances brought competition, warfare, absorbtion, amalgamation etc. amongst the different ethnic tribes. The defeated or weaker tribes were not in a position to easily move away from the Manipur valley surrounded on the same altitude by different mountain ranges. Their habits, customs, occupations, language etc. were found to be almost similar because of their common practices. These situations definitely provided a favourable condition to absorb these communities and intermingle with those defeated or weaker tribes with the victorious clans. Thus, the *Meitei* civilization is the gift of the barrierless geographical position of the valley. It is amalgamation of many cultures and historical traditions brought by different communities into this region.

To a greater extent, the pristine Meitei State developed through different structural phases. When the structure reaches at its apex, a new social phenomenon i.e. conquest or warfare one of the important reasons for the birth of a State, come to appear. Of course, when the population increased, agricultural and habitational areas were short in supply. On the other hand, the surplus production was highly essential to the clan Ningthou or chief in order to meet managerial requirements of their respective clan principalities. Generally, the control of surplus production became the basis for acquisition of political power. Therefore, the clan chiefs would often desire of new territories or more wealth (i.e. control of cultivable land, cattle, local population etc.). Probably, the defensive pose of their respective territories would become the common objective of the clans. Such atmosphere brought frequent conflicts among the clans.

According to Herbert Spencer:

> "the inter-societal conflicts i.e. conquests caused forceful permanent subjugation of defeated group and the compounding of society which are the important factors in promoting centralisation of the regulating agency."[24]

The *Khabas* (a powerful clan group) defeated Nongda Lairen Pakhangba. But very soon Pakhangba with the help of Moirang king retaliated and smashed the power of the Khabas. Many of them fled away and took shelter in the hill areas and with Puleiromba of Angom principality respectively. Khaba Nongampa surrendered to Pakhangba. Soon after it, Pakhangba confronted Poireiton, who had marched towards the Imphal valley. Poireiton finally accepted the suzerainty of Pakhangba.[25]

After a prolonged struggle against his own kinsmen, the Khabas and Poireiton, Pakhangba the first historical Meitei king ascended the throne of Kangla with great support from the Angom chief Puleiromba, Luwang chief Langba Langmaiba and Mangang chief Apanba. Other tribes and the leaders of the Chakpas also accepted his suzerainty. The successful war against Poireiton and the Khabas, the coordination of Puleiromba, Langba Langmaiba and Apanba and the acceptance of Pakhangba's supremacy by many tribes and the Chakpa leaders brought a high degree of subordination within his own territory and outside his kingdom and increased manpower.[26] Only the Khumans and Moirangs were left out of the Meitei confederacy. Socially, they were brought under the fold of the Meiteis, though the political autonomy was maintained by them for several centuries.[27] Thus, the early Meitei State was moulded under the iron hand of Nongda Lairen Pakhangba.

Generally, the climate of Manipur can be described as a monsoonal one, characterised by annual rainfall of the prevailing wind directions separated by the two transitional seasons. The monsoonal rainfall regime is regarded as one of the dominent factor to decide the fate of the Meitei civilization. The valley of Manipur has been a lowland type and it slopes southwards so that all the major rivers of the valley run towards south and all join each other on the middle or lower regions of the valley. Usually, the valley of Manipur is divisioned into three regions like peripheral belt, good bottom land and lake region. The rivers and dozens of lakes and streams of Manipur considerably have provided fishing ground and transportation facility. Due to receive of enormous rain, in the past the entire valley almost faced the problem of innundated flood water in every year. This situation practically compelled the rulers of Manipur to develop up the idea of management of water. Essentially both ecology and topography certainly made profound influence on technologically less developed inhabitants of early Manipur. This intimate relationship between environment and technology became more significant than other types of culture influences directly on the ancient inhabitants of Manipur to engage in different occupation.

The clan people in the beginning were in all probability highly concerned regarding water bodies and depended highly on nature. They benefited from the natural water bodies. Therefore, they selected the water body areas as their habitational ground to get transportation, daily use of water, fishing and gathering facilities. In different pre-State periods, the clans like the Mangang, the Luwang, the Khuman, the

Khaba-Nganba, the Sarangleishangthem, the Chenglei, the Angom, the Moirang, the Thanga-kangbong etc. came to rise either on on the banks of the river valley or near the lakes. In a specific case, clan capital area was connected with the surrounding places through canals. All the clan principalities enjoyed both the lake and reverine facilities.

The Luwang principality appeared to the western part of Lamphelpat and on the banks of the Luwangyi river. Angom clan enjoyed the Kongba, the Iril river, the Yaranpat and the Porompat (lakes). Moirang principality installed on the bank of the Moirang river and the Loktak lake and also enjoyed the facility of the Khuga river. Thanga-Kangbong settled on the bank of the Waishel river. It got the facility of the Wuphongpat. Khuman principality developed on the bank of the Imphal river or the *Turel Achouba*. It would get the facilities of the Loktak, the Khoidum and the Kharungpat lakes.

The growth of clan principalities was relatively influenced by their respective natural locations. The immediate tasks of the clan people were to exploit and mould nature for the welfare and development of clan societies and also to wage war against each other in order to protect their clan land, procure power and more wealth. Since they settled on or around the lakes and river banks, they engaged various waterborne activities for their benefits. The clan people less capacity to construct good land roads. Most of the time, they used lakes and river as their transportation routes. For owning fishing lakes, frequent clan internecine warfare took place. Such circumstances ultimately led to organized naval power. The most eventual example was Khuman-Moirang conflict. Their main conflict was to establish their sphere of influence on the Loktak lake. The Loktak was very useful to both principalities because of its wider geographical extent, its innumerable natural resources of livelihood and advantageous transportation facilities. No doubt, Loktak lake was regarded as a launching pad of the Moirangs to expose their outside clan-world. Definitely, both the Moirangs and the Khuman principalities built naval force to achieve their aims. Probably their mutual aggressive postures compelled these clan chiefs to organise their respective man power and to make a number of trunk boats. To a greater extent, such organizational patterns brought people together to make a powerful clan principality and propelled them on the way to State power. These aspects also led ultimately to State-formation in not so distant future.

During the reign of Luwang chief Shapaiba, Lamphel Shoy was established. They planned it not only to catch plenty of new and fresh fish but also to entrap animals. He was responsible to dig two different pesciculture canals. One canal was for pesciculturing of Ngaroi fish (*Crossocheilus burmanicus hora*) and the other was for Ngatel fish (a kind of fish).[28] *Mkubi Shoy* (weir) was built under the complete supervision of Luwang Salai Hanba. It was particularly prepared for fishing. Nambul Shoy (weir) was given to Yumburembi of Kanglei as dowry, when she was married to Thangyi Ningthouba of Luwang. They had three sons Pathang Ahanba, Yunaorei Yaimaba and Naoremton. The management of this Shoy (weir) was handed over to their eldest son Pathang Ahanba. The two types of fishing such as *Aka Shoy* (fishing during the flood season) and *Akum Shoy* (fishing during the winter or dry season) were done in aforementioned *Shoy* in two alternative seasons. During the rainy season, various number of fishes were caught in this *Shoy*. Another form of fishing like *Akum Shoy* was carried out during the winter season in which particular *Ngashep* fish (*Mystus bleekeri*) were caught in such *Nambul Shoy*. Later on, the right of management of this Shoy was passed to their youngest son Naoremton at the instigation of his mother. However, *Nambul Shoy* was given different names i.e. *Lumpu Shoy, Hekap Shoy, Heshotpan Ngashep Leikang-Ee, Akum Lairak-Ee* and *Lanloi Chingareng Khamla Loukhong Shoy*.[29]

At Kanglei Wakhei Kon of Turel Langmei Pung (Heipok river), there was a *shoy* owned by Theba Nahakpa. The Kanglei chief exercised his power over this *shoy* (weir). He allowed Heirem-Khunjam clan women to catch fish at Heipok river. Khaba Shokchrongba also fully prepared to catch fish in this river.[30] Heirem Khuncham erected a *'Pn'* or dike across a canal fallen into *Konte Patt* or lake. Here, he created a shoy by using *Kharai* (made of kniting bamboo piece). *Meital shoy* was owned by Thing Konpa, a youngman of Heirem.[31] The chief of the Heirem was responsible to make Heirem Nongyai Khong canal mainly for fishing purpose. This canal was also known as Ngakha Khong on account of abundant catching of *Ngakha* fish *(Puntius puntio)*. This fishing canal was developed typically. When a cow went through it, cow's tail did not touch the water of this canal; when a pig crossed it, the entire body of the pig could not be covered by water of canal; when a dog passed over it, dog's belly did not touch canal water.[32] It was mainly meant for allowing the fish to grow and multiply in this canal. It developed as an indigenous method to culture fish.

Khuman Nongyai Napanpa dug a canal (Khong at Thoubal. It was created to store water for daily use. Lokha canal, Nongyai Leishang Khong (canal) and Khoupubakhong khong (canal) were excavated under the supervision of different *Khuman* personalities like Aton Nongyai Lokcha Heipa, Leishapam Moipa Phap and Nongyai Khoupuba.[33]

Kainou Chingsomba of Angom clan made Chingsomba *khong* (canal). Chonmeibi and Chonmeiba, these two soldiers dug Chonmeibi-Chonmeiba *khong* (canal). Khamtoubi and Khamtouba created Khomtoubi-Khamtouba khong (canal). The four canals (*khongs*) such as Chongsomba *Khong*, Kanglatombi (present Imphal municipality) Khonglen Yai, Chonmeibi-Chonmeiba Khonglen Yai and Khamdoubi-Khamdouba Khonglen Yai were joining each other to Paota Hiden of Turel Achouba or Imphal river near Kangla.[34]

Moirang, an ancient principality situated on the bank of great fresh water Loktak lake territorially stretches from Khoiriphaba area of Nambol and the boundary between Kha-Jiri and Waroi Ching hill in the north to Wangu in the south and from Manipur river or Pumlenpat and its surrounding like Mondum hill and Lokha-Houkha in the east and Matarok river and its surrounding hill, Thingjing ranges and Khuga valley in the west.[35]

In the beginning Thangjing Koirel Lai, the first *Ningthou chief of Moirang* governed the Thangjing ranges. Of course, they came down to the foot hill and expanded their settlement to the river valley and the bank of the Loktak lake. Such development encouraged them to establish a strategic capital at Moirang Leikoi Pung. The newly installed capital was encircled by Moirang river in the east, Thangbotek river in the west, tributary of Moirang river in the south and Hyenkhong river and the confluence of Thangbongtek river and Moirang river in the north. The capital was in position to protect from easy intrusion of the enemies inside the palace area.[36]

It is worth to mention that Kanglei Phathiba used to address Moirang principality as *Khongna Hemthoiba* (decorated or surrounded by a number of canals) and its chief was also addressed as *'Laija Eshingna Wangba or Henba Laingee Mapu Oiba Hea Ningthou'* (O! King owner of the land or principality dominated by water body).[37]

The Moirangs set up their habitational area in the lake area by making settlement mound since the early period. The best example is that Nganta Sirai Kangcha of Moirang begun to dwell in the lake area by creating a higher settlement mount.[38]

Moirang chief in order to administer his principality amicably, organised manual labours to conduct various water work programmes such as making canals and water ways and establishing fishing 'Shoy.' Nganba Serai Kangcha of Moirang excavated Haotangkhong canal to provide daily use of water to his subjects.[39] During the reign of Puriklai, fishing 'Shoy' (Weir created across the canal or stream to catch fish) was established at Ungamel near the confluence of Khuga and Manipur river. It's main object was to catch plenty of fish. Ningthou or chief Puriklai Miyom Michaoba of Moirang unearthed Moirang Nongkangkhong at Khoiritak particularly to trap animals.[40] In order to facilitate fishing, he initiated to set up Laphu Kumtam shoy (weir). Keke Kokpa Naoremkhong Huithouba canal was built for fishing purpose. Chief Yoirel Tompokpa accomplished to create Khuyon Pengba shoy not only to catch Pengba fish (*Osteobrama belangeri*) but also to get water transport facility.

Toiyal canal was built mainly for boat transportation.[41] Sanathoibi Shoy located between Khuman clan and Heirem Khuncham clan territories was owned by Kege Moirang Leima Angom Ningol Sanathoibi.[42] By carrying out welfare public water works, Moirang chiefs could attract the massive loyalty of his subject. Besides, the people of Moirang regarded their chief as the descendent of their supreme god *Thangjing*.

Having thought to incarnate as a *Eshing Khonglam* (*Eshing* = water and *Khonglam* = canal or drainage) to this being world, Chingu Khoyum Ashiba better known as god Sanamahi sent seven women goddess: *Chitnu, Thamnu, Arenu, Ahumnu, Tetnu Tainu, Thonthongnu* and *Thareloybam Chanu. Chingu Khoiyum Ashiba* (who had one thousand eyes, feet and hands), soon came out on the earth. He was named as 'Laija Eshing Ongthi.' From such eshing water, seven drainages arose. These are Kumshu Khong, Phisukhong, Tumukhong, Taobikhong, Nongdamkhong, Charoikhong and Muwakhong which were very helpful in draining water from the low lying areas and for transportation. *Chingu Khoyum Ashiba* one of the great worshipped gods of the Meiteis, was virtually responsible to develop and maintain the drainage system around the Kangla hillock.[43] Thus, he was ever associated with the development of Kangla. He was gradually personified as God but initially he was a social worker with reforms on his mind.

Purum Khonglem Ching or Kangla hillock had its seven ranges. Naturally, it was surrounded by different lakes i.e. Kekrupat, Akampat,Porompat, Nungjengpat, Hichamyai champat, Uphongpat and Lamphelpat.[44] The height of Kangla was about 2619 ft. above the sealevel. Seven streams arose from these ranges and drained out their water in the surrounding lakes and rivers.[45] Besides, there were other nine *khonglams* (canals) namely Khakhong, Laikhong, Mrakhong, Lilhakhong, Phisukhong, Charoikhong, Yambikhong, Manungkhong and Nongdamkhong. The term '*khonglam*' (Khong - canal and lam - line or road) is identified with canal.[46] It can be estimated that these canals were dug out to drain the water of the lakes and swampy areas. On the other hand, the aforesaid canals were excavated to establish link between Kangla and the surrounding lakes and rivers which were connected to other far flung areas.

Khakhong canal was created to join Imphal river and Keishampat lake. Laikhong canal linked Imphal river and Lamphelpat lake. Both Merakhong and Charoikhong canal were dug to join Porompat lake and Imphal river. Lilakhong canal was unearthed to link Imphal river and Hichamyaichampat lake. Yambikhong canal was created to link Kekrupat and Imphal river. Theso interlinking of rivers and canals shows the ingenuity of the valley people to retain a sensible flow of rain water from one region to the other. (It is already stated that the valley had increased rainfall during the rainy season.)

From time to time Kangla hillock was leveled down by the Meitei kings. It was during the reconstruction period of Manipur, Gambhir Singh initiated to flatten Kangla hillock[47] about 7 ft. Probably, it is alleged that greater part of Nungjengpat, streams, canals, ponds river beds etc. found inside the geographical limit of Kangla were filled up by the sediments. The process of filling these areas were hastened by the human activities. However, Kangla became the most attractive habitational area of the valley. It developed as an equidistant place from north, south, east and west points of the Imphal valley. The proper and amicable hydromanagerial works launched by the chiefs or kings highly correlated to let Kangla emerge as a spiritual cosmic centre of the Meitei concept of Universe. It is designed as the source of political power of the Meitei. It is also believed that 108 abodes of deities reside inside the Kangla. It surprised the people. Nungjengpat continued to be preserved as a sacred pond where Pakhangba the most celebrated first godly Meitei king dwelt to regenerate spiritual and political power.

The process of Leishemba i.e. creation of Kangla and its development started several years ago took comfortable shape, when Khagemba (A.D.1597-1652) diverted *Turel Achouba* or Imphal river's course from west to east of Kangla-hillock by cutting a canal. Palace enclosure was surrounded by small brick walls. Thus, the ancient palace of Kangla was completely fortified by the river in the east and brick walls in the west, south and north. However, earlier drainage system existing around the Kangla declined due to diversion of the Imphal river. The old course of the Imphal river gradually got fill up.[48]

Meidingu Khunjaoba (1652-1666) grabbed Thangapat or the moat canal around the capital to strengthen the defensive aspects of the capital. For the first time, it was rounded by the canal in the north, south and west.[49] He further properly refilled the old course of the river. During the reign of Garibniwaz, under his direct supervision, the Thangapat or canal constructed by his predicessors was systematically repaired and old course of the Imphal river was also replenished once again. King Marjit by organizing large number of human labour made outer moat of Kangla. Two ponds were completed to dug and these were inaugurated with ritual works. Another remarkable development was to extend the boundary of Kangla eastward beyond the present Imphal river. He demarcated the eastern boundary of Kangla by digging a new Thangapat or canal at Khurai area. He also initiated to create a canal from Sanjenthong to eastward Nongmeibung.[50]

In 1857, the north *Thangapat* or canal from Sanjenthong east of the Imphal river to Khurai area was excavated by king Chandrakirti. This enabled to bring a complete demarcation of the fortification of Kangla, east of the Imphal river. In 1878, a long canal from Iril river to the eastern *Thangapat* or canal of Kangla was excavated in order to provide water transport facility to his subject. The people inhabiting on the bank of Iril river and beyond it, could now sail directly upto Kangla through the newly made canal without any hindrance. Such gigantic water work not only enhanced the power and prestige of the king but also drew massive loyalty of his subject. A canal which interlinked the Kongba river to Porompat lake was excavated. The main aim of the king was to make a water regulation system that led to control both, lake and river water, in time.[51]

Comprehensive defensive works were usually carried out by the Meitei kings around the capital. Such corresponding works would be definitely determined by its natural location. Since it situated an equidistant places of different points of the valley, the possession of Kangla was considered as the most prestigious and powerful act. The plan of defence and control of strategic Kangla became an eventual factor in emerging State situations.

During the clan period, frequent warfare took place among the clans like Angoms, Khabas, Mangangs and Chengleis to capture Kangla. Even after the formation of the Meitei State, the State was frequently challenged by its neighbouring principalities, i.e. the Khumans and the Moirangs, sometimes by the other tribes and foreign powers. It order to make Kangla a formidable one and to protect it from the surrounding aggressive neighbours, it was highly necessary to fence Kangla. In the beginning Kangla was surrounded by the Imphal river in north, west and south and by a lake and canal in the east. Later on, during the reign of Godly king Khagemba, the palace itself was fortified by defensive brick structure. Further the capital area was fenced by the inner and outer *Thangapat* (moat or canal) in the west, north and south and river in the east. An available literary source and the existing archic canal clearly indicate that the proto-Meiteis and the Meiteis settled in Manipur, were equally effective in making both, hydraulic systems and military constructions develop. War prisoners were impelled to create a number of defence canals. The Meitei kings were always inclined to use the rivers as a means of defensive means. Chandranadi river dug by King Bhagyachandra was designed to defend the Canchipur capital. Another new Imphal river course from Minuthong to Shanjenthong was cut under the initiation of king Khagemba to use it as a river-fort of Kangla. These canal operations clearly vindicate what Karl A Wittfogel states that:

> "even primitive hydraulic societies could achieve in the field of defense construction when they strained their cooperative resources to the full."[52]

The mechanism of hydraulic power and the mechanism of developing water resources all go hand in hand in developing political control and State powers.

After the foundation of the pristine Meitei kingdom by conquest, the stability and State apparatus was brought under the stress of certain circumstances like religious and hydromanagerial works. Traditionally, the Meiteis were the wet rice agriculturists since the inception of their settlement in present Manipur valley. They primarily practised low land wet rice cultivation with broadcasting. However, the full-swing expansion of the Meitei State followed the wet rice cultivation by transplantation method. The success of cultivation entirely depended on seasonal monsoon rains. The cultivators collected rain water by making *Louri* or rectengular ring (made of clay and mud). Besides, the villagers constructed *Thingels* (dikes) along with the course of streams and then water was brought to the cultivable fields through *Loukhongs* (canals). Sometimes, the Meitei kings involved in the construction of bigger *Thingels* (dikes) to prevent violent floods. During the reign of Gambhir Singh, at Leishangkhong a *Thingel* (dike) was made along the river course of Thoubal river. On the other hand, in the upper reaches of the Kakching or the Sekmai river, the *Thingel* (dike) was built under the care of Kakching Ningthou, Budheraja, to provide water to the fields.

The periodical monsoon rain caused seasonal violent floods which destroyed the planted fields and affected also the low-lying settlement areas. In order to prevent them from eventual flood, river water control was highly essential. Hence, the king undertook programmes of dredging rivers and draining swampy areas. The ancient literary text *Tutenglon* (History of dredging river) clearly explains that both, the royal brothers Ngangoi Yoimongba and the king Yoiheiton Taothingmang dredged *Turel Achouba* or Imphal river and Iril river. It is learnt that both brothers organized large human labour groups including women to carry out such gigantic work.[53] These welfare measures were highly applauded in the valley society.

"In the course of the dredging, as soon as they arrived at Lilong, a man by the name of Phunal Telheipa told them that they could not dig the river in his land. So, the elder brother, Yoimongba turned westward and continued digging when his younger brother Taothingmang arrived at Lilong and asked Phunal Tenheipa how long it was since his brother had left, he was told that his brother had left quite a considerable time ago. To this, Taothingmang asked if he could take a short cut through his land. This was refused by Phunal Telheipa saying that Taothingmang was forbidden from going through his land. They fought each other; but king Taothingmang was hurt by arrow shot by Phunal Telheipa. Then Taothingmang left to follow his elder brother and caught up at Lokkha Haokha, a village of Thoubal."[54] The main objectives of digging and dredging of rivers was not only to control flood but also make an effective river transportation system. Achenkhong canal was mainly built for water transport. Meidingu Taothingmang sailed in his war boat often through the canal to overpower his enemies.

During the reign of king Pengsiba (379-394), a frequent occurrence of flood caused great havoc to the people of Manipur. In order to check such violent floods, the king started to take up the plan of deepening the bed of Imphal river in the valley. He also carried out the diversion in the upper reaches of this same river at Thingba Karong to the river Gwai (Barak) in the Maram hill area of the kingdom of Manipur.[55] Bunds were also constructed by king Naokhamba (411-428 A.D.) at Yaorei Khumpilok in the upper regions of Imphal river to check flood in the valley region.[56]

Chingbi Leima *khong* or canal was called after the name of Keireima wife of Meidingu Naophangba (428-518). There is a story for naming the cited canal as a Chingbi Leima *khong* or canal when the wife of the king was trying to catch fishes by using fishing net, Laiba Ungam Thaba sailed his raft towards the direction of her fishing area. It created waves and disturbed her plans to catch fish. All the fishes nearby the fishing net suddenly went to hide amidst reed and under water. Therefore, she rebuked him that she would not possible to catch even a single fish. If she returned home without bringing any fish, she would be denounced by her husband. Having got intentiton to say something, Laiba Ungam Thaba replied that he would not sail further. Then, he moved up on the bank of the canal and waited till the end of her fishing. It is reliable that Chengbi Leima or Laiba Ungam Thaba canal would provide both transport and fishing facility of fishing of transport.[57] When the Sheeloi-Langmai forces entered the kingdom of Urakonthouba (568-658) without his consent, they crossed a fishing shoy or Weir at a marshy lake area. It was managed by a servent of the king. He enjoyed both '*Aka Shoy*' and '*Akum Shoy*.' It was named as a Khabei Pung *shoy* (fishing weir).[58]

During the kingship of the Meidingu Thawanthaba(1195-1231) Nongchup Merakhong canal was created. It ran in the western side of Kangla and served the purposes of draining water and transport. Some of the war heroes like Nakhuba Nakubi and Haoba Thikaba were captured here as a prisoner. They were forced to dig Merakhong canal.[59] Cheirei Siyankhong canal was made under the direct supervision of the Meitei king Thingbai Senhongba (1242-1247). Both, the Meiteis and the Khumans used to sail their boats in this canal. Hence, Cheirei Siyankhong canal was important for their transportation. When king Loinai Khumomba (1263-1278) waged war against his enemy, Chanamkhong canal was dug mainly to store water for daily use.[60] By defeating his enemy, Meidingu Moiramba (1278-1302 A.D.) arrested Phutapi and Phutaba as war prisoners. Both the prisoners were forced to create a *shoy* (fishing wier).[61]

Meidingu Tabungba (1359-1394) unearthed Ahingkhong canal (near Kalimai-Imphal) over a night to defeat the powerful Kege or Moirang. Hayingbi and Hayingba of Kege were captured as war prisoners. He occupied a village and the villagers were forced to dig Shanglou Keipha Khong canal. This canal was put to use for trapping tigers. Under the direct care of Thingpaingambi mother of Meidingu Kambomba (1524-1542), a canal named Thingpaingambi Khong was excavated.[62] King Ningthoukhomba's (1432-1467) wife Leima Ningthoingambi was highly concerned to dig Shaya Khong which was specially to entrap various animals.[63]

Without getting exhausted, the Meitei kings continued to work on the water managerial programmes. Lainingthou Khagemba paid more attention to the welfare of the State and its people. The king constantly drained water from the swampy and marshy regions by digging canals to reclaim more settlement and cultivable lands. Queen Lengnaomonbi, wife of Meidingu Khagemba dug Chakppa Pumshaikhong canal by organizing the entire people including women and children of the village. Meitei Leima Koubaron Taipongambi took part to consider with her husband, Khagemba to catch fishes like Pengba and Ngawa easily, whenever they needed. With this idea, she initiated to dug fishing canal called Leima Taipombi Lemlei Ngayok khong. Another queen named Leima Sanarembi of king Khagemba involved herself actively in building Charei Pheinkhong canal mainly to perform Ahong Kumhei or festival. More or less, the Meitei queens played a decisive role enhancing kingdom's economy which led to the making of a strong State apparatus. Yaikhu khong was used for an offensive purpose against the Thongnang village. The particular village was occupied and it's leader Putaptao was arrested as a prisoner. He was compelled to excavate this canal. Another canal i.e. Tachai khong was grubbed up during the reign of Khagemba by a prisoner named Patakol of Thongnang Mayang village.[64]

When the Cachari Muslims under the rebel leader Sanongba, younger brother of king Khagemba invaded Manipur, Meidingu Khagemba dug a long canal extending from Phumlou to Toupul. Such a canal was particularly for defensive purpose.[65] During his reign, under the supervision of Ebungo Nongthonba a stone dike or *Pn* was constructed at Mayanglam to make an effective wall to control flood around the valley area. The King himself was highly sensible in providing transporation facility to his subjects by digging Kyang Khong and Takhel Khong canals.[66]

The large scale water work programme undertaken by king Meidingu Khunjaba brought a systematic development in the water-transport system of the kingdom. From Chinga of Singjamei to Thangmeiband, a big canal later known as Nambul river was dug during his kingship. The opening of this cannal marked a new chapter in the anals of water transport system of the kingdom. It is only the canal directly interlinked between the Khwairamband market and Loktak, the greatest fresh water lake of Manipur. It's link would reach as far as the southernmost part of the valley and it was the most busiest inland water transport route of Manipur several years before till the middle part of the 20th century. Since it extended upto Thangmeiband, it definitely connected the Naga stream. Moreover, the new development pattern enabled the people to carry on trade between the Khwairamband market and different places of the northern and the southern regions of Manipur. Drainage was dug around the Khwairamband market. The king created Ngaprum *Pn* or wier specially to catch *Ngaprum* fish (*Monopterus albus*). During his kingship Imphal river was blocked by making a dike at Sanjenthong in the month of *Poinu* (December and January) in order to preserve water. Sometimes, the kingdom would face the scarcity of water during the dry season due to long absence of rains. Such situations compelled the king to take up certain device i.e. water management programme to solve the impending problem and often he had to perform the prescribed rituals to beget rains. As an usual routine, the *lallup* labours were assigned to carry out such inevitable welfare public work under the constant vigilent eyes of the king. It is estimated that the welfare water works itself provided the real mechanism to gain the loyalty of his subject. He also drained the Naga stream and built dike along the course of this stream in the month of *Hiyangei* (October and November) of 1661 particularly to check the flood. He further made bunds around the Khwairamband market to arrest the innundation by river waters.[67]

Meidingu Paikhomba opened Loklaobung *thingel* or dike in the month of *Wakching* (January and February, 1683) to draw off water which was stored during the rainy season, from the low-lying area to Imphal river. In 1684, the Naga stream was properly blocked and as soon as possible the lower course of its bed was dredged to deepen it. He refitted the bank of the Imphal river from Singjamei to Thongju in the month of *Wakching* (January-February). It was a pre-plan preparation of King Paikhomba to check the river flood in these areas. It was during the reign of Charairongba that a dike was made at Eharai Waikoksung and a drain was also dug up in the month of *Phairel* (February). Imphal river at Khurai was also excavated to deepen and straighten the river course.[68]

In March 1718, Maharaja Garibaniwaz undertook the programme of draining of Imphal river at Singjamei. In the same month both Naga *thingel* (dike) and Kaya *thingel* were constructed to store water. The digging up of Kha-Khong seemed to have disappeared, upto Imphal river it was once again dug out. By organizing the entire people of Keirup, Waithou *thingel* (dike) was constructed at Waithou river in the month of Poinu (December). Moirang Lanhaba Yumthangba dug the river which runs through Mayang Laimanai area (The area inhabited by the slaves of Queen) and the work was extended upto Laishangkhong area. The four panas or divisions successfully carried the repairing work of the Imphal river from Kona Konchin to Koirengei. River transport route at Mongsnagkei was dug up under the supervision of the king himself. In the month of Langban in 1738 (September), the king launched a huge programme of digging earth at Sagolband and created a new canal extending from Naoremthong to Nambul canal near Khwairamband market. The Nambul river which runs southward direction was diverted to eastward by cutting a new canal at Sagolband. The newly created canal became the course of Nambul river and it provided a water transport facility to the people inhabiting the areas nearby the canal.[69] Most of the people of the kingdom were organised by the king to involve in repairing works for the kingdom. King Garibaniwaz himself took the responsible to start such work in the month of Hiyangei (November) in 1741.[70]

An irrigated canal was dug at Yaorou. A part of these dedicated welfare water management for the first time became State concern and it started to pay attention to profitable welfare water works. The State being the owner of the land distributed cultivable land according to the will of the king and his convenience. The new changing domination of regime attributed more loyalty, more burden of tax; tightening of state's grip over the cultivated fields. King Garibaniwaz won decisive battles against the Kabaws or the Shans, the Takhels and again the mighty Burmese empire etc. The power of the kingdom of Manipur attained it's zenith and Garibaniwaz became an unparalleled military general. Besides, he posed himself as an innovator. King Garibaniwaz continued to work upon Imphal river from Kona Konjin to Leishangkhong. Under the leadership of Keirungba further repair work was conducted on the river from Phibou to Phabakchao. Moirang Khema was sent to grub up Poireikhong canal. King got the Ningthem Pukhri pond dug up to store drinking water. Another pond was also dug at Kongba.[71]

During the reign of Maharaja Bhagyachandra, Heipok water route through Mayangningthou Nai area was dug under the supervision of Chingakhamba Tangkhomba and Hinaohanba. A new river was dug at Canchipur. It is stated that from Mongsangkei to Khajingkhong, Nambul river was drained. In 1782 a pond at Langthabal was dug. Under the order of Anantasai, Keiroilakpa Malti (noble) by organizing seven Keiroi lineage, dug Lamlongei pond. In 1783, Anantashai Jubaraj led the entire people of the kingdom to involve in the construction of dikes at Iril river of Ethem Chingjin area. The main object of making it was to check river flood. It was completed within nine days. The bank of Naga stream was drained. Besides, king was responsible to get the pot holes filled up and weak areas of Imphal river beyond Lilong area. By organizing entire people of the kingdom including *Loi* + *Nai* (Loi- outcaste community + *Nai* - servant). Bhagyachandra deputed *shanglakpas* (nobles) of the four *panas* (division) to dig Chandranadi from Chaumkei to Lamangdong. The work was finished within two months. The Kabuis of the hill area were organized by the king and they were assigned the repair work of Chandranadi river embankments. From Koirengei Imphal river was drained to regularise the flow of the river. By organizing the entire people of the kingdom, Maharaja Bhagyachandra initiated to dig a canal named Leishang Hithen. Its main object was to make a proper place of the boat race.[72]

Presumably, the continuous welfare public water works conducted by the Meitei king were the regular mechanism to cultivate loyalty as well as support of their subjects. As his predecessors did, Maharaja Modhuchandra begun to grub up a pond at Langthabal capital. In 1811, Imphal river was blocked by building dike across the river to store water. An irrigated canal which extended from Kyamgei to Hyen Khong was created to supply water to the paddy fields. Meirenkhong canal was also repaired. In 1842, king Narasingh drained Imphal river to make a regular flow of river. The reopening of a river course which runs inside the Kyang Engkhol area was taken up under his supervision. The King went to look after the work of making dike across the Imphal river at Khumidok village in the month of *Engel* (July) particularly to restrain flood. The people of the thirty-two hill villages i.e. Awanghao, Laisham, Tora, Chawai, Shomtan, Phatang, Khunthak, Toinem, Kachai Okkhram, Huining, Hundung, Choithar, Heichum, Nungshong Khunkoi, Shanthak Kashom, Khamlang, Nimpui, Shokpao, Chapang Heini, Loiyi, Kashong, Shakoklang, Khamping Meiring, Tusom Chompi, Hangkou Ngaprum, Nungman Nungou, Pheijom Tongou and Shoukapung were organized by the king and they were assigned to excavate the river bed inside the Kiyang Engkhol area to regularise the flow of water which had been hindered by sediments and the fallen mud embankments.[73]

In 1857, all the tribes of north of Manipur were assigned the digging of water transportation route extended from Angom Louwai Chingaren to Khabeishoi area. Sana Thoumanbi stream which falls already in the Kangbung agricultural fields was diverted to Leimakhong cultivable fields. Luwangyi river was drained by the tribes of the north of Manipur. Of course Thiyam pat was transformed into *ningthem loukon* (cultivable land owned by the king) and *chingphu loukon* (cultivable field) was developed. Phabakchao canal and Ingourok irrigated canal were respectively excavated. A number of ponds like Yatpokpi pond, Yumjao pond, Wangon pond, Keitenbi pond, two ponds of Govinda were drained one after another. Under the direction of Loitongba Subedar water transport route extended from

Maklang to Eroishemba Chingjin.[74] Naoremkhong canal at Khongjom and Ngangoukhong canal were constructed.[75]

The pristine Meiteis extensively undertook number of non-agrarian hydraulic works to store for daily use and drinking water. By utilizing limited primitive technology and available materials constructed a number of temporary dikes across the rivers and streams mainly during the winter or dry season to store and supply drinking water. Normally, the Meitei kings had a full knowledge of making permanent ponds inside the palace compound and thickly habited villages to conserve usuable water.

All the rivers and streams which run in valley are short and small. These rivers from the surrounding hills which cannot be compared with those of the permanent snow capped mountains are short in supplying enough water to the local rivers during the dry season. Though Manipur receives heavy rain, during the dry season water level of the river flow in the valley gets reduced and sometimes seems to dry. For such reasons comprehensive installations across the irrigular and regular flow of rivers and streams were established to crop up river water easily. Besides, the people planned to collect rain water by digging reservoir ponds at personal levels.

It is significant to explain that during the off season water from the lakes, swamps and marshes were drained through the canals and the streams to make convenient for cultivation and settlement. Presumably, a low-level *Pn* (dike) was built across the rivers and streams were made by using clay, wood and bamboo. When the innundated water backs through the canals, with the help of big and small '*Shouraru*' (a kind of cone-shapped tool made of bamboo) and cane pieces, different varieties of fish were caught abundantly. Such system of catching fish is known as Shoychaba who looks after the work of fishing of the *Shoy* area (where the *Pn* or fishing wier constructed across the canals or streams). The Shoy system was divisioned into *akashoy* (done during the rainy season when the water level increase) and *akumshoy* (done during the winter season when the water level decrease). Some of the important *Khongs* or canals dug under the initiation of the State are Nongmaikhong, Ungamel Marin, Nganan Marine, Komnakhong, Phabakchao Khongin, Shamushang, Maramba Marine etc. *Shoys* (weirs) were set up in these aforsaid canals.

There were number of the stream such as Irumbi stream of Naransena, Moirang *Turel* (river), Yangoi *Turel*, Langkambi Marin etc. which were maintained by the *Shoychaba* (who looked after or owned of fishing weir) particularly for fishing purpose. With the introduction of *Patchaba* (*Pat* = lake, *Chaba* = person who look after the protected lake area) system, some portions of different lakes of the kingdom were made as a protected fishing area. Thus, the Meitei kings collected fish as a revenue in early, medieval and late 19th century from reserved lakes and State own shoys. An organized fishing system was an inevitable task of the kings to maintain proper economic condition of the kingdom. Fish is a compulsory preferable suplementing-diet of the Meiteis. So the Meitei kings actually involved in making fishing shoys, canal, to catch plenty of fish.

Primarily hydromanagerial work necessiates some basic mechanisms like maintenance, personal quality and organizations. The water control programme brought to thrive centralized organisation of large human labour under a single authority. Such pattern of organization was usually done by amicable kings whose sole responsibility was management. In case of the Meitei kingdom, only the rulers were successful to do such work.[76] However, the Meitei kings were not only considered as competent organisers but also regarded as tactful managers. The hydromanagerial works successfully tended to strengthen the centralised power of the king. Moreover, the Meitei kings were able to draw the massive loyalty of their subjects. Then mechanism of controlling water was instrumental factor to bring peace and development of the State. On the other hand, the water work programme became an important role in integration which was brought by the large scale participation of the people in the network of construction of dikes, draining and dredging and digging of ponds and canals. Success in water controlling work led to generation of wealth of various kinds and greatly enhance State's pride.

Since Manipur was ecologically a hydraulic State so regular water management programmes became a compulsory task. The geo-physical knowledge of the Meitei kings and their active response to mould the surrounding environment became a harmonizing centralized feature of the kingdom. Their sole object was to nurture the State. Probably, the frequent and continous participation of the masses in the secular public work like water work, attributed the sense of integration and loyalty which developed the idea of responsibility. The Meitei kings were highly conscious about the topography of the kingdom. Soon after the establishment of the Meitei kingdom, Nongda Lairen Pakhangba ordained all the able bodied males to render service for the welfare work of the State. However, this rudimentory form of labour organization was legalised by king Loiyumba who introduced the *lallup* system. *Lallup* labour was organised to utilise various State works like war, construction of houses, bridges, roads, canal, draining rivers, digging ponds, etc. The *lallup* (Lal = war and Lup = organization) service as applied to every male between the ages of 17 and 60 of the kingdom. People were obliged to perform public works for only ten days out of forty days.[77] It was an institution sponsored by State for the welfare of the kingdom. The *lallup* service was applied to whole population of kingdom. The following thirty days, the common man was allowed to remain at home without bearing any burden of *lallup*. If a man failed to appear to his assigned *lallup*, he was liable to forfeit one rupee and for this a substitute was hired. The absentee 'Lallup' could make a bargain for his substitute. The substituted person received seven of four rupees. "In cases where the men of any area found that the work imposed on them was beyond their powers it was possible to call in men from the whole area till the work was finished."[78]

According to Colonel McCulloch:

> "the population of Manipur comprised of different classes. The principal was the Meiteis, next the Phunganai, after whom the Tangkhul, the Ayokpas, the Kei, the Loee and the Musalman."

The Meitei population was organized by dividing four

divisions named *pana* which were designated in the order of their superiority. *Khapam, Laipham, Ahallup* and *Naharup*. The *panas* were liable to perform *lallup* service for ten days in rotation. Thus entire male population of the kingdom above 16 years were organised to do State duty. None are remunerated for it. With the introduction of this *lallup* system, the head of each family or tribe was responsible to furnish the proper persons for different sources required of that tribe. The immediate family of the *peepa* (head of the tribe) is not called upon to carry out any heavy duty. In the family the person next in seniority would have heavy duty to perform in the Leikai or lane. The third was the *lalmee* (armies) and the fourth the *sangsaroi* (house builder). The 'Lallup' of the second and the fourth families worked generally in unison. Their chief duty was to make houses and bridges for which they cut and brought the materials. Of the families after the fourth, the place were not fixed. All the remaining classes had their lallup service in which they did any work in their respective lines.[79]

Sometimes, those people i.e. war prisoners, beyond the geographical limit of *lallup* service were compelled to dig canals. The Meitei kings like Tabungba, Moiramba, Khagemba etc. impelled the war captives to build canal. Whenever they needed they called upon all the able bodied males and even women. The Meitei king Taothingmang with his elder brother Yoimongba organised all the population including man, woman and children to drain the *Iril* and *Turel Achouba* rivers. Queen Lengnomonbi, wife of Khagemba organised the entire people including women and children to make canal. Maharajas such as Bhagyachandra, Narasingh etc. also organised all the people to carry out the work of draining rivers. Hence, the Meitei kings levied and controlled the required labour forces adopting systematic method. The hydraulic Meitei rulers were sufficiently strong to do organizational work on a national scale through a well established institution i.e. *lallup*. The Meitei kings fulfilled a variety of important managerial functions. They maintained many hydaulic and non-hydraulic works like protective enterprises, defensive measures, fishing places and water storage schemes.

In his two articles published in the *New York Daily Tribune* in 1853 as a consequence of journalistic criticisms of British foreign policy, Marx investigates to study the Asian societies. Marx framed a new model of Asiatic societies based on economic dimensions. His advocacy for the economic aspect of Asiatic societies were primarily conducted around the new concepts of Asiatic system of landownership and Asiatic mode of production.[80] He highlights to discuss the relationship between the concept of early State and his new idea of Asiatic production. His new model of study made impact around the globe. It profoundly influenced the Asiatic students who devoted to study their respective societies, to do deeper investigations. For better understanding of such relationship, it is worth discussing briefly the characteristic features of Asian Societies advocated by Marx:

(i) Oriental or Asiatic Despotism or the Character of Asian State,
(ii) Absence of Private Property,
(iii) Village Communities and forms of Communal Property,
(iv) Village Communities and Economic Self-sufficiency, (v) Trade and Towns and
(vi) Stagnation, Stationary and changeless.

Oriental or Asiatic Despotism or the Character of Asian State

Marx characterized Asian State as despotic and hypertrophied State. He primarily expressed concerns about the Asian State through geographical and climatic factors. He believed that the arid lands of Asia cannot be brought under cultivation in a wider scale without irrigation canals and water works. Usually, the village communities were unable to organize separate association to undertake large-scale irrigation. Therefore, such large scale irrigation was undertaken by the king or government. The successful irrigation/water work attributed the existence of centralized powerful despotic Asian State. This developmental relation caused the emergence of dichotomic relation between agricultural communities and the State organizations, occasioned by the necessity of constructing and maintaining irrigation systems.

Absence of Private Property

Marx understood that in Asia, the direct exploitation of producers living in village communities was not based on private landowner but mostly work under the direct dependence on a despotic ruler the head of the State. The surplus product of these communities was appropriated in the form of taxation by the government so that ground rent and taxation coincided.

Village Communities and forms of Communal Property

Marx discovered that a basic feature of the Asian village communities was the communal property in land. He believed it was an early social formation. The formation of Asiatic despotism was based on communal property. In this form, the individual had the right of possessing the right to work on land. The individual was not an owner in separation from community but the individual was only the owner of a particular part of it. Consequently, the individual existed in direct unity with the community. Thus, numerous village communities embraced despots who appeared as the sole proprieter of all land.

Village Communities and Economic Self-Sufficiency

The Asian villages were self-sufficient and self-contained and these possessed arable and waste lands of their own, resulted to form a little world in itself. Marx explained that the circle of production was self-sustaining, unity agriculture and craft manufacture was described as a basic feature of the Asian property form. He asserted that the self-sufficiency and isolation of the Asian villages were further strengthened by their independent and separate political and social organization. Both Marx and Engels pointed out that these self-sufficient village communities were the fundamental social formations of Asiatic despotism.

Trade and Towns

Marx believed that in Asian Society, there were absence of internal commerce, independent merchant capital, and commodity production and exchange. The important part of the products of the village community was destined for direct use by the community itself. This community production did not take the form of a commodity which was not entered in the market. As a result of it, the division of labour was confined to non-commodity products. He thought that within the village, the craftsmen enjoyed an unchanging market. Basically, they were unable to get a change to produce more. It helped to develop division of labour like that in the manufactures in case of the growth of population. Such development did not lead to the rise of the market but it led to the establishment of a new community an unoccupied land with its own quota of non-commodity producing craftsmen and servants. In Asian society, there was a lack of separation between town and country in the development of exchange of commodities. Marx assumed that in such Asian societies a large part of the rural produce went to the State and became a commodity (i.e. the surplus production was paid to the State as rent in kind not in cash).[81]

Stagnant, Stationary and Changeless

Marx postulated Asian society basically as stagnant, stationary and changeless. The society ever remained on the stage of primitive communism. He stated that the absence of private ownership of land made social stagnation in Asian Society. He assumed that there was no periodic changes in the political organization of Asiatic society from dynasty struggles and military conquest, and in such societies there were no radical changes in economic organization due to the ownership of the land and organization of agricultural activities which remained with the State as the real landlord.[82]

It is not an easy task to bring an Asiatic society within the framework designed by Marx's model of Asiatic Mode of Production. But it envisages the idea of rethinking, when one studies about Asiatic society. The wholesale application of Marx's general characteristic features of Asiatic Society to every early societies of Asia would not favour in any condition. It will not be in a wholesome way appropriate to study the pre-capatalist Meitei society within the Marx's structural design of Asiatic Mode of Production. Undoubtedly, the pre-capitalist Meitei socio-economic system had no exact counterpart in Marxian economy of Asiatic Mode of Production. So, the Marxian Oriental or Asiatic Despotism discussed in his Asiatic Mode of Production isunapplicable to Meitei society; because the specific features of Marx's Asiatic Despotism has diferred from the Meitei despotism which retained a weak character.

According to the Marx, irrigation was an important device of the emergence of Asiatic Despotism. His emphasis is that the arid land of Asia could not be brought under cultivation in a large scale without artificial irrigation. The village community separately or in association could not carry out large scale irrigation because of the vastness of territories and low level civilisation. However, such work was not taken up successfully by the State and it led to the existence of the powerful and centralized Asiatic despotism. Whereas in Manipur, there was limited cultivable river valley and lake regions. Usually, wet rice cultivation was widely practised because of her geographical and climatic factors. Probably, the necessary water was supplied by the rains. Small scale irrigation was undertaken by the villagers themselves.

Till the first half of the 18th century in Manipur, there was no any State own irrigated canal. When king Garibaṅiwaz ascended the throne, he for the first time, dug one State owned irrigated canal. The State would not pay more attention to take up large scale irrigation programme because of receiving plenty of seasonal rains. Still the villagers displayed a dominating role to practise field irrigation by manipulating streams. The Meitei Kings were rather to pay more attention to those of the non-producing hydraulic enterprises. Though the king was the sole owner of the land, every citizen of the kingdom was authorised to own at least some portions of homestead area of land. More or less, Meitei society was self-sufficient and self-sustained and it was class based society. Every villager had also communal land area where individual villagers were not separated. Besides, they had separate private cultivable lands through reclamation. The pristine Meitei society underwent changes due to eternal factors and external pressures. Peasants were independent producers as well as main tax payers. Internal trade was fairly done without monopolistic atmosphere whereas external trade was too limited and seasonal. The selling and purchasing were entirely based on barter system. However, king was responsible to establish market centres. However, the surplus production of grains was restrained for the Meiteis preferred to have only one crop pattern all over the State prior to the coming of the muslims and even after that land use pattern was rather defective.

REFERENCES

1. E.R. Service, *Origin of the State and Civilization, the Process of Cultural Evolution*, New York, Norton, 1975, pp.36-37.
2. Lewis Henery Morgan, *Ancient Society*, New Delhi, 1986, pp. 9-12.
3. Henri J.M. Claessen and Peter Skalnik (eds),*The Early State*, New York, the Hague: Mouton, 1978, p. 7.
4. Manners R.A. and David Kaplan, *Theory in Anthropology, A Source Book*, Chicago, Aldine Publishing Company, 1973, p.256.
5. T.B. Bottomore, *Sociology a Guide to Problems and Literature*, New Delhi, Blakie & Son (India) Limited, 1975, p. 180.
6. I. Amubi, N. Khelchandra, O. Bhogeshor, N. Ibochouba (Compiled) *Sagei Shalairol, Meiteigi Yek Salai Yumdaba Puya*, Imphal, Manipur,State Kala Akademi, 1994, pp. 29-30.
7. W. Ibohal Singh, *The History of Manipur (An Early Period)*, Imphal, Manipur Commercial Co., 1986, pp.575-6.
8. *Ibid.*
9. Gangmumei Kabui, *Hisoty of Manipur*, Volume I Pre-Colonial Period, New Delhi, National Publishing Home, 1991, p. 71.
10. Venice to John Wilmot, *The Encyclopedia Americana*, vol.28, New York Americana Corporation, 1829, p. 121.
11. O.Kumar Singh, *Archaeology of Manipur*, Imphal, 1983, pp.7-9.
12. F. Houtart and G. Lemercincir, *The Great Asiatic Religions and their Social Formation*, New Delhi, 1984, p. 10.
13. Gangmumei Kabui, *op. cit.*, p. 87.
14. W. Ibohal Singh, *op. cit.*, p. 332.

15. *Ibid.*
16. B. Kullachandra Sharma, *Ancient Principal Tribes of Manipur with special reference to Plain Tribes*, Seminar on Ancient History of Manipur held on 21-6-87 at J.N.Dance Academy Hall, Imphal.
17. W. Ibohal Singh, *op.cit.*, p. 339.
18. N. Ibochouba Singh, Thiren Mairam Leeba, Imphal, 1982, p. 20.
19. E.R. Service, *op. cit.*, p. 78.
20. M. Chandra Singh, *op. cit.*, p. 5.
21. Romila Thapar, *From Lineage to State*, Bombay, Oxford University Press, 1984, p. 5.
22. E.R.Service, *op. cit.*, p. 78.
23. R.Cohen and E.R.Service, *Origins of the State: The Anthropology of Political Evolution*, Philadelphia, 1978, p. 30.
24. E.R. Service, *op. cit.*, p. 24.
25. Gangmumei Kabui, *op. cit.*, p. 83.
26. *Ibid.*
27. *Ibid*, p. 84.
28. Moirangthem Chandra Singh, *Panthoibi Khongkul*, Imphal, Manipur Sahitya Parishad, 1972, pp. 21 & 24.
29. M. Manaoyaima Singh (transcribed), *Chengleiron*, Imphal, Manipur Sahitya Parishad, 1979, pp. 22-23.
30. Moiranthem Chandra Singh, *op.cit.*, p. 44.
31. Oinam Bhogeshor Singh (transcribed), Toreirol Lambuba, Imphal,Manipur State Kala AKademy, 1984, pp. 23 & 27.
32. *Ibid*, p. 24.
33. *Ibid*, pp. 64 and 69-71.
34. *Ibid.*, pp. 83-84.
35. M. Nodiachand, *Moirang Salai*, an article presented to S.R.Institute sponsored Seminar on History of Manipur before 1500 A.D. held at Imphal in 1985, p. 8.
36. *Ibid.*, p. 9.
37. Ch. Hemchandra Khaba (transcribed), unpublished, p. 4.

38. Oinam Bhogeshor Singh(transcribed), Moirang Ningthourol Lambuba, Imphal, 1983.
39. Ch. Hemchandra Khaba, *op. cit.*, p. 5.
40. *Ibid.*, pp. 20-21 and O. Bhogeshor, *op. cit.*, p. 42.
41. Ch.Hemchandra Khaba, *op. cit.*, pp. 29-30 and 36-37.
42. Oinam Bhogeshor Singh, *op. cit.* p. 26.
43. Sairem Nilabir Singh (reproduced), *Laining Nat Amasung Puwarigi Mityengda Kangla*, Imphal, 2007, pp. 26-27.
44. Somorendra Chongtham, *Hiyang Hirel, Kangla-Sha and Kangla (Ashinachingba Manipuri Shangkritka Mari Leinaba Hiramshing* Khomjinba Wareng, Imphal, 2007, p. 31.
45. Hijam Chanu Phajabi (transcribed), *Kangla Nunglon Laiphamlen*, Imphal, 2005, p. 2.
46. Somorendra Chongtham, *op. cit.*, p. 30.
47. Moirangthem Chandra Singh, *Gambhir Singh Nonggaba*, 1967, Poknapham Publication, Imphal, p. 20.
48. Lairenmayum Ibungohal Singh and Ningthoukhongjam Khelchandra Singh (transcribed) *Cheitharol Kumbaba*, Imphal, 1967, pp.24,26 & 27.
49. *Ibid.*, pp. 32-33.
50. *Ibid.*, pp. 90-91 & 216.
51. *Ibid.*, pp. 340 & 436.
52. Karl A. Wittfogel, Oriental Despotism, A Comparative Study of Total Power, New Haven, Yale University Press, 1957, p.36.
53. N.Manaoyaima Singh (transcribed), *Tutenglon*, 1986, Kakching, pp.2-5.
54. Saroj Nalini Arambam Paratt (translated), *The Court Chronicle of the Kings of Manipur,* Routledge-Tylor and Francis Group London and New York, 2005, p. 23.
55. O.Bhogeshor Singh, *Ningthourol Sheireng*, Imphal,1967, pp. 221-22.
56. N. Angou Luwang (ed), *Pakhangba Nongkarol*, 1983, Imphal, p.27.
57. Chanam Hemchandra Khaba, Kangleirol (An account of different places of Manipur with important historical events), Imphal, 1996, p. 20.

58. Ch.Manihar Singh (translated), *Naothingkhong Phambal Kaba*, Imphal, 1983, p. 7.
59. Ch.Hemchandra Khaba, *op. cit.*, p. 75.
60. Ch. Hemchandra Khaba(transcribed), *Toreirol* (unpublished), pp. 75 & 105.
61. *Ibid.*, pp. 69-70.
62. *Ibid.*, pp. 97, 131-132.
63. Chanam Hemchandra Khaba, *op. cit.*, p. 100.
64. *Ibid.*, pp. 35, 67, 70, 92 & 96.
65. R.K. Sanahal Singh, *Pangal Thorakpa*, Imphal, p. 7.
66. L. Ibungohal Singh and N. Khelchandra Singh, *op. cit.*, p. 28.
67. *Ibid.*, pp. 32, 34 & 35.
68. *Ibid.*, pp. 40, 48, 53-57.
69. *Ibid.*, pp. 68, 72 & 93.
70. *Ibid.*, p. 96.
71. *Ibid.*, p. 86.
72. *Ibid.*, pp.110, 127, 128, 130, 138 & 158.
73. *Ibid.*, pp. 173, 207, 263 & 265.
74. *Ibid.*, pp. 336, 338, 359 & 450.
75. M.Gourachandra Singh, The Manipuri Topologmy (A Treatise of Place Names in Meitei) 2004, pp. 310-11.
76. Heisnam Nilkant Singh, Early Political System of Manipur and Thailand, Imphal, 2006, p. 26.
77. R. Brown, Statistical Account of Manipur (Reprint), Delhi, 1975, p. 83.
78. T.C. Hodson, *The Meitheis* (Reprint), Delhi, 1997, p. 61.
79. Major W. McMulloch, *An Account of the Valley of Manaipore*, Calcutta, 1959, pp. 11-12.
80. Tom Bottomore (ed), *A Dictionary of Marxist Thought*, 108, Cowly Road, Oxford, O.K 4, J.F.England, p. 29.
81. Bipan Chandra, *Karl Marx, His Theories of Asian and Colonial Rule*, Centre for Historical Studies School of Social Sciences, Jawaharlal Nehru University, New Delhi- 110057, pp. 7-30.
82. Tom Bottomore, *op. cit.*, p. 33.

3

Rice Culture and Social Formation in Manipur

Topographically Manipur is divided into hill and plain. The hill area is characterised by high elevation, steep slopes and river running areas. The valley comprises the central bottom land area and like region which covers low-lying marshy and swamp areas. Between the hill and plain, there is good gradient area since the absence of river valley in the hill region is free from flood. The most parts of the valley areas enjoy both, rain and flood water. According to Pemberton, the fertility of the soil of the valley area is so great that the crops generally prove most abundant.[1] Manipur is marked by tropical climate with hot and wet summer and cold winter. Her climate is advantageous to promote rice cultivation.

The main theatre of Manipur civilization is around the valley. In A.D. 33 the small Asiatic Meitei kingdom was founded by Nongda Lairen Pakhangba. The kingdom was physically within the fold of South East Asia. The South East Asian kingdoms are broadly classified into maritime or commercial kingdoms, land based agricultural kingdoms and bureaucratic kingdoms. The early South East Asian States had a tenuous institutional base and were transitory in nature as passing leaders or arrival of challenges created new areas of concern and authority. Almost all the State of this region flourished on the river basins and deltas and those might be tabled as subsistence model. Such type of States have different programme to support themselves.

Largely, there were self-sufficient communities who produced and engaged in different ways of trade, fishing, cattle rearing etc. in order to sustain themselves. The basic type of the primary Meitei kingdom can be categorised as land based agricultural or river basin kingdom. In its initial stage the kingdom attained politico-military power, though it remained small in geographic size. Though the State was engaged in wet-rice cultivation deeply, the control and supply of the necessary water for cultivation were largely managed by individual farmers and were heavily dependent on monsoonal rains.

In Manipur, a number of prehistoric sites such as Songbu Cave, Khangui Cave, Open air site of Machi, Tharon Cave, Napachik , Funan, Nongpok Keithelmanbi exist.[2] Various sites experienced changes in different phases of the prehistoric period. The availability of charred animal bones clearly indicate that Manipuri culture had developed sufficient knowledge of using fire.[3] However, the presence of a large number of batter marked pebbles and small pebbles reveal that the Hoabinhian people of Nongpok Keithelmanbi might have had some idea of rushing food.

Both Palaeolithic and Hoabinhian cultures were based on hunting and gathering economy. In Manipur the archeologists have unearthed a number of Neolithic sites such as Nungpok Keithelmanbi, Napachik and Funan villages. Various types of Neolithic tools and potteries have been discovered from these sites.[4] The presence of various types of potteries such as cordedware, tripod and geometric designs in some parts of the hill and valley are glaring examples of the promotion from nomadic to settle life based on domestication of plants and rudimentary type of agriculture. Not only the archaeological findings but the Meitei *puyas* (Chronicles) also provide some information of the cave dwellers. Thirel Layat *puya* mentions the cave dwellers whose livelihood was dependent on hump and they used bark as their dresses.[5] Another Meitei *puya Sakok Lamlen* also records the proto-Meitei inhabitants who used hump, hunted animals and gathered food from the surrounding forest.[6] According to Kangbalon *puya* refers that King Kangba of Mangang clan was born in the cave of Koubru hill in northwest of Imphal valley. The livelihood of his subjects depended entirely on fruits and plants, animals and streams of hill.[7]

In addition to their hunting and gathering culture, the Neolithic people would have developed the knowledge of plantation of various vegetables i.e. *pan* (Arum), *ha* (yam), pumpkin, guards, *mangra* (sweet arum) etc. Neolithic pebble picks discovered from the Neolithic sites of Manipur are important tools for planting different vegetables. Probably, the domestication of vegetables is regarded as a commencement of field agriculture. The Neolithic people of Manipur started to establish their settlement on small hillocks and hill ranges which stand in this valley and the peripheral foot hills. The important Neolithic village settlements are Napachik a small hillock located at Wangu of Bishnupur District, Nongpok Keithelmanbi is situate at the peripheral foot hills of Senapati District and Funan settlement site stands on the Funan hill of Imphal East District. Since they had the knowledge of domestication of various plants and cereals, the neolithic people would claim their vegecultural fields through mainly burning and cutting of forests. Though, the neolithic village settlement is registered as rather sedentary settlement, the villagers shifted their vegecultural area after every few years to be close to new areas while previously planted areas were left fallow.

With the expansion of settlement in the valley areas, there was a techno-physical change took place. The proto-Meitei society of course, grew and expanded due to increase of population which standardized of tools. Food gathering was still quite dominant. However, the folk-tales of the Meiteis witnessed the exploration and use of paddy. *Wainu Chara* (a variety of rice) which was found abundantly in the lake region of Manipur could grow suitably either in swamps and lakes, but the flowering of this crop is seasonal. It clearly indicates that the forefathers of the Meitei had sufficient knowledge of using such wild crops as a paddy since the inception of their settlement in present Manipur valley.

According to *Kangbalon puya* (chronicle), rice humps were plucked from the trees at Wakonthoi Chakson Pung. Salt was also collected from Thunambi. Both fish and meat were also found having from the trees.[8] Thus, during the reign of king Kangba of Mangang clan was in the stage of active food gathering. *Numit Kappa* (the ancient text) refers to the clear cut existence of agricultural community during the clan period. The use of paddy was known to the people. In order to restore normalcy, *Ningthou Pongba Tara* (ten regional chieftains) went to search *Nongdamhan* who had fled away from the capital on hearing the news of shooting of *Taohuireng* by Khwai Nongjengbam Piba, on their way they came across a woman folk who planted paddy in the field.[9]

According to *Kangbalon Puya*, King Kaksuba reclaimed a swampy lake area called *kakwa* to make agricultural field. During his reign agricultural lands of the field were maintained by slaves. Their engagement of slave labour in agricultural purpose was to enable the expansion of field agriculture. Probably, the construction of permanent agricultural fields also marked the development of wet rice cultivation. The art of cultivation was quite simple. People used mainly spade to dig the field, but swords and axes were also used to clear fields. In spite of reclamation of permanent agricultural field, shifting cultivation was widely practised. The farmers adopted the slash and burn method in their shifting fields. Panthoibi Khongul mentions the practice of *pamlou* (shifting cultivation).

When the proto-Meitei began to settle on the present valley of Manipur, soon they would have experienced the art of wet rice cultivation. Though scholars have failed to find out the exact first rice-growing place on the earth, it is believed that monsoon regions in South East Asia would be the home of rice. Manipur lies within the tropical South East Asia and definitely it's climatic condition and topography provided the favourable condition to grow wild paddy. Incidentally, wild paddy was found in several parts of early India in Bihar, Bengal, Orissa, Madhya Pradesh, Andhra Pradesh, Assam etc. Also at several places a blackish, purplish paddy was also reaped.

However, there was a great interesting event of exploration of wild paddy from the lake region of Manipur. During the reign of King Tonkonba, a kind of wild paddy called *morshi thangii* was discovered at Akampat east of the Imphal river near Singjamei. King Puthiba also paid a great attention to agricultural development. He was deeply engaged in agricultural activities and always spent to search the fertile cultivable areas. Even his two daughters. Shoubon Leima and Sana Khongnang Leima were asked to cut down the trees in order to prepare cultivable fields. During his reign, a new era of development in field agriculture got inaugurated with the invention of the plough and the yoke. The beak of *Wainu* (bird) was commonly used as a plough. The successful tilling of the soil by using beak as a plough would make a plentiful production of rice.[10]

When *Poireiton* (a leader of a colonizing ethnic group and a contemporary of Nongda Lairen Pakhangba) entered Manipur, he brought not only different varieties of paddy such as *chahao, fongnu liksi yaiphou*, but also agricultural implements and domesticated animals etc.[11] Therefore, with the coming of Poireiton, there was a considerable change in techniques of cultivation and standard production of paddy. Such development benefited the newly established Meitei kingdom. To a greater extent, the people practised rather wet rice cultivation in their respective permanent cultivable fields than shifting cultivation.

King Taothingmang and his younger brother Yoimongba organized a large number of human and dredged both Imphal and Iril rivers successfully.[12] Taothingmangs's programme of dredging marshes of the Manipur valley and dredging its river and streams brought to expand the cultivable areas and to control the seasonal flood. Besides king was able to cultivate the strong sense of loyalty of his subjects. *Ningthourol Lambuba* refers that during the reign of Naothingkhong wet rice cultivation was deeply persued by the valley people whereas shifting cultivation was mainly practiced by the hill dwellers such as Shelloi Langmais.[13]

Another dynamic change in the sphere of agriculture took place during the reign of King Khagemba. In addition to *pumhul* (casting dry seeds in dry fields) and *pamphel* (a new transplantation method of cultivation) was introduced. The Cachari Muslim war captive peasants were responsible to renovate the cultivation system by introducing plough pulled by either bullock and buffalo. Large areas of agricultural land were also reclaimed by draining swamps. King introduced a new kind of paddy known as *taothabi* which was very suitable to grow in the low-lying areas. Generally, this kind of paddy is planted to the seasonally inundated or flooded fields because it consumed much water and depleted the minerals etc.in the soil. During the dry season all the inundated areas of lakes and flood plains of valley are often found dry. The seasonal flood rejuvenated the soil and made them more fertile. These aforesaid areas were suitable place for *taothabi* paddy. King Khagemba initiated to dug *Kyang Khong* and *Takhen Khong* to drain water from swamps and low-lying areas. He also constructed bunds to control flood.[14]

Since time immemorial, water is essential for being used in different ways. But the primitive people of Manipur did not understand the methods to manipulate natural water bodies and so they had little need of water-control, when they were in the stages of food gathering, hunting and fishing. Only after the commencement of field agriculture, the reproductive process of the plain lives became visible. This instance coerced the pristine Meiteis to learn the utilization of water in their planted fields. They collected water by using various means to utilize in the fields. Hence, water became an essential natural prerequisite for successful crop raising.

Historically, as the population of Meitrabak (ancient name of Manipur) moved from gathering and hunting to a more sidentary existence, permanent village communities emerged. Agricultural mode of production influenced the hill and village structures of Manipur. In the early period, in the hill areas slash and burn vegeculture was commonly practised. Generally, fields were defoliated through the cutting of bushes and burning the residue on the field so as to add nutrients. Villagers moved every few years to be close to new fields, while previously used fields were left fallow. Fallow periods varied with general soil and ecological conditions and more importantly with population pressure.

The first appearance of the new Kukis in Manipur during the reign of Narasingh clearly indicates the sudden change of demographic structure of the hill people. Thus, the population pressure became another major factor in hastening the change of new fields and the increase in the number of villages. In addition to their vegeculture, they began to get engaged in *jhum* cultivation. Rain water was the only means to grow their cereals. The period of cycle must be five to ten years. The ecological balance of slash and burn agriculture is such that it could only sustain sparse populations. Slash and burn in hill villages varied throughout the region. Some groups like the new Kukis were nomadic in habit and were moving all of their belongings with them while travelling over hill areas, whereas other like old Kuki and Naga maintained permanent communities preferably on hill tops. A considerable change takes place in later period that in the hill area, "near the banks of the river and in the small strip of valley, permanent cultivation was carried on and most of the hill-men had to depend entirely upon their jhum cultivation on the slopes of the hills. The mountain land around the village within the certain fixed bound was usually the property of the village."[15]

It is believed that from the earliest time, the *Tangkhuls* used to settle on the crest of a hill. They mainly selected their village site where abundant water source existed. Having got a definite village boundary of its own, the Tangkhul village land was classified into the following categories:

(a) village site,
(b) cultivable site,
(c) Public land,
(d) Grazing ground and
(e) Forest land.[16]

According to R. Brown, unlike the Naga tribes, the Kukis were constantly changing the sites of their village to suit the exigencies of their cultivation. On this account the villages of the Khongjais were not that permanent. The village site got altered according to the kind of cultivation near them.[17]

In the valley area, there were certain areas which were permanent agricultural fields like broad flood plains of primary and secondary river systems and around the lake region. Traditional Meitei communities deeply engaged in wet rice cultivation. But the necessary water for their cultivation was mainly received from the streams and rains. The villagers for their better convenience of cultivation created *Louri* (a rectangular mud ring made of mud and clay in their respective agricultural areas to collect rain water). Besides, traditional Meitei agriculturists created many *Loukhongs* (irrigated canals to make an easy access to water from the streams.) By using their limited tools like spade, sword and axe, the villagers could raise dikes across the streams. Thus, water was stored by blocking stream current. They usually cut main *loukhongs* to make a direct connection to streams and have access to the loaded water to main *Loukhongs*. Several other smaller *Loukhongs* were also created separately by the villagers in their own respective expenses to bring water directly to their own field. The farmers together owned the main *Loukhong* (irrigated canal). It is customary for cultivation that under their local level of understanding, they coordinated among themselves and transferred plentiful and accessible water supply from its original location to their cultivable areas through their main or smaller *Loukhongs* (irrigated canal). These water management enterprises made an identical position of the State. The State was the owner of the land and it was regulated by the king. Some were made grant to officials, favourites, sometimes for their own lives, descendents,[18] gods, goddess, meritorious military heroes individuals, sepoys etc. These lands might be transferred hereditarily. In short, the peasants owned land freely; but they were liable to pay tax to the State either in kind or money.

None of the pre-Garibaniwaz literary and historical texts mention about the construction of State-sponsored irrigated canals, though the Meitei kings manipulated cultivable landscape by draining water from the marshy areas and swampy lakes. New arable fields sometimes were reclaimed. Probably, the access of water from the streams were completely left to the village cultivators. Therefore, for many years in Manipur, irrigated canal water management which was the basis of the Oriental agriculture an outstanding device of Asiatic Mode of Production, was not controlled by the State. The traditional Meitei cultivators primarily managed their water management job within their settlement limit.

Manipur received enormous rain from south west monsoon. The required water for cultivation was fed by the monsoon rains. According to T.C.Hodson:

> "the innumerable already which gush from the bases of the ranges surrounding the valley ensure an adequate irrigation, even to the fields which are above the level of the general inundation."[19]

Manipur is also within the heaviest rainfal zone of the world and its general topography and thick forest also cause to receive heavy rainfall. "That in the 19th century the annual rainfall of Manipur was 142 cm."[20] The prevailing rainfall regime not only influenced in the State to pay more attention to the management of surplus water caused to make frequent floods in the valley, than the field irrigation but also make healthier situation for the cultivators to collect water for cultivation in their own ways.

Probably, landholding is interrelated to the primary mode of production in the village communities. The wet rice agricultural villages hold more wider areas of land than the jhuming villages possessed. Though the State was an absolute owner of land, an individual families were also given the right to hold some parcel of land. By dividing the villages of Manipur into *Siphai* (soldier) and civilian villages, the king had given the right to the *Siphai* villages to get one *pari* of land per head from the land around their villages free of revenue and provided some facility to the civilian villages also to hold one *pari* (two and half acres) of land around their villages but they were to pay land revenue.[21] Apparently the villagers were main tax payer as well as the labour suppliers to the State. In every village, community-owned land was found. The important communal lands are namely grazing ground, forest land, playground, cremation grounds and fishing areas. The extension of communal owned land was depended on the reclamation of more fallow land. The extension of communal cooperation beyond the immediate family became an instrumental devico of meeting needs and achieving goals.

While the actual task of ploughing was usually undertaken by one or a few individuals, the plantation, the clearing of the agricultural fields and harvesting were left to team or a group of people. With the introduction of field agriculture, animals were widely used in cultivation.

As far as concern about the soil of rice fields, the people tried to improve or renew soil by adopting different methods. It is an usual arrangment of the farmers that when they mowed the paddy plants, they left a considerable portion of straw. After about three or four months, the field was ploughed and the remaining straw decayed. Probably, such process helped to enrich the soil of the field. Deepening hoeing and digging of fields assisted in making more fertile the cultivable areas to a certain degree. The new reclamation of paddy fields were not needed either to renew or improve the fertility of the soil because of virgin soil of these areas. For annually innundated low-lying areas, there was no any question of deficiency of soil. According to R.Brown:

> the soil of the valley was nearly all throughout of excellent quality and of great depth.[22]

Pecularities of her wisdom of politics, gifted martial qualities or tactful martial qualities and her topographical structure allowed the Meiteis of South Eastern track of Himalayan regions, to set up its State society amongst the head-hunters. Both offensive and defensive aspects became an eventual task to safeguard the Meitei civilization. On the other hand, the State is properly maintained by adopting various devices. However, the political economic and geographical features became the major factors to form socio-economic structures. The system itself could survive this civilization for many centuries in the borderland region of the present Indo-Myanmar territories.

Occupation was the foremost reason which brought the development of social formation during the pre-Meitei State. According to the existence of different production systems, (like shifting cultivation practised during the neolithic period which continued for many centuries), low land-rice cultivation by broad casting, (it was practised since the clan period to the Khagemba period) and wet rice cultivation by transplantation (it was started to engage from the time of king Khagemba) different social relation emerged. Generally, the capacity to produce vegetables and maize by shifting method was decreased by the requirement of frequent move to virgin land where the reeds were planted. All the necessary water was fulfilled by rainfall. The yield under this system was not plenty. Direct and simple relation among the individuals were the common feature and the production system was also primarily controlled by the individuals. Possibly most members of such society must have been acquainted with all forms of primitive economic activities such as fishing, hunting food, gathering, agriculture or vegeculture. The shifting cultivation would not have fully developed a primitive mode of production. Due to frequent shifting of their vegecultural shifting fields, any pattern of land tenure either as private property or as clearly specified communal property was found absent. The situation was not in a position to build a social formation upon its own material advances. Consequently, a base line social formation would have possessed on the rudimentary class based on sex and age.

However, the lowland wet rice cultivation was performed to the permanent fields with the expansion of habitational areas in the valley regions. Such method of cultivation needed much water than the shifting varieties. The requisite water qualities of this cultivation was mainly provided by monsoon rains. In order to distribute fairly and timely, either rain or stream water control was highly needed. The corresponding relation among the villagers themselves and between the king and his subjects were clearly identical, when the water management works were carried out.

Agriculture as the basic work that appears for the regular surplus of production further allowed to develop material foundation for social formation in the valley. Once surplus production got regularised, political ruling class also tended to emerge. Usually, this ruling class became the determinant factor to bring a sudden change in any social system of pre-State society. During the clan period, there were subsequent warfare which took place among the clan principalities. The defeat of the Khabas at the hand of Nongda Lairen Pakhangba practically brought in existance a State society in which the king was the sole owner of land. He definitely controlled production units as well as labour. It also exclusively allowed a military class to exist which was regular. Since the reign of Pakhangba, all the able bodied persons were liable to render military service to the State at the time of war. The small population and the lack of production forces could not feed the regular militia. It seems that in the initial stage of Meitei State formation the indirect social relation emerged. This new social relation was unable to develop sufficiently to match the Meitei social formation during the initial stages. Soon, the situation changed and the ruling power comparatively increased due to the success of labour organisations and control of more productive forces.

The central power organised peasant labours who were engaged in secular public works like draining water, digging dikes and dredging rivers. Generally, two main class structures distinctively came to exist in the early formative social formations. The ruling class consisted of a king and his nobles and the commoners including peasants and slaves remained a subservial group. Most of whom were undoubtedly rice agriculturists and fishermen. Perhaps, there were a few specializing in carpentary groups/ethnic communities, craft and tool-making works etc. Besides, some peasants may also have specialised in fishing, gathering of forest products, weaving dyeing, silk manufacturing pottery making, dye making, basketry,canery etc.

With the foundation of the Meitei Kingship, there was appeared rigid dynastic succession. A single dynasty was only allowed to ascend the throne. A number of royal families formed the ruling class. Such circumstances signify the constitution of ruling class in the Meitei social formation. Thus, the distinct structural class of ruling family became pivotal to set up or corelate with other classes of society. *Loiyumba Shinyen*, the royal edict, clearly mentions that the ancient monarchy of the kingdom of Manipur was fully established due to presumption of a political leadership, socio-religious head, innovator of economy of the kingdom etc. During his reign, there were some evidence to indicate that the social relations of the kingdom were more advanced than those of the earlier periods. King's control over labour became more systematic and rigid. Greater productive activities also expanded with the feudalization of handicrafts and industries. These resulted in making more advanced social formations. The situation could enable a full utilization of peasant labour in various socio-economic activities. The stratification continued to increase with the allotment of different socio-economic and religious functions of the people. There was a tremendous development in the sphere of handicrafts. The edict of *Loiyamba Shinyen* further mentions that as many as 30 families were allowed to weave various designs of cloths and they were divided into weavers and dyers. It is also precisely recorded that 101 families of *maibas* (priests) were assigned to perform different duties relating to the sick, the rites and the rituals and the birth and death ceremonies.[23]

Gangmumei Kabui observes that during the reign of Loiyumba:

> "the agrarian economy was now supplemented by the growing handicraft industry."

The emergence of the artisan class was a great landmark in his reign. The people who were essentially peasants, had become artisans and had started rendering feudal service of *lallup* to the king."[24]

Further stratification of ancient Meitei society took place even during the reign of king Kayamba, when the immigrants like Brahmins from the mainland India and Shans of Upper Burma, were absorbed in the Meitei society. The shans were completely amalgamated in the Meitei lineage system, while the Brahmins were given local girl in marriage and they formed a separate social group.[25]

Significant changes in different spheres developed during the reign of king Khagemba. A new method of transplantation of rice cultivation was introduced. A systematic preparation of field demands more labour highly needed to transplant rice successfully. This developed a new social relation known as *khutlang* (Mutual assistance). It may be summarized that the production system of the early Meitei society fulfilled slightly above the minimum required for the subsistence of the population. Perhaps, only a small surplus was produced (which in earlier centuries generally met the king's requirement or demand). This seems to be a paradox since the formation of a State requires more surplus production so that the State treasury could be enriched for payment of wages to labourers and officers of the State for varities of duties and works.

As many as 31 lineages were not only given to the Cachari Muslims war captives and they were also allowed them to settle in low-lying regions of the valley.[26] Thus, the situation indicates the emergence of new stratification of Muslim labour class in the Meitei society during the kingship of Khagemba. The practice of both rice cultivation with broad casting and transplantation, introduction of new variety of paddy (i.e. Taothabi very suited to grow the low-lying swampy areas) and the birth of a new stratification of labour class not only indicated the full development of productive forces but also appeared to be a product of a surplus production. The engagement of water managerial programme for agrarian and non-agrarian and the elaborate labour organization programme were relatively associated to exist and form another pattern of social relations of production.

During the prehistoric and proto historic periods, the valley of Manipur served as the best harbour of various ethnic groups, while in historical period, it was related to neighbouring States in India, South East Asia and China. Nevertheless, the Meiteis distinguished themselves by building up a State society developed through its traditional socio-political and economic structures and warfare. The knowledge of wet rice or field agriculture was a vital reason to transform the valley settlers from primitive simple society to a complex form of society.

It is highly essential to highlight the different segments of the early Meitei society, when one discusses about the emergence of the Meitei social formation. The earliest social groups were individuals, family and lineage. Generally, family was the basic smallest unit of the kinship system of the Meiteis. The Meitei society was patrinial in character, hence father was regarded as the head of the family. When the sons got married, according to the convenient or condition of the family they either relieved from the main family or lived together with the parents. The married persons were supposed to share all the affairs of the family. In case of the death of the male head of a family, the widow grand-mother and mother were fixed the responsibility of the family. The married women took the maximum share of the affairs of the family. Inasmuch, the Meitei enjoyed both single and joint family. A small family consisted of parents, sons and daughters, whereas a larger or joint family comprised of grand-parents, parents, sister-in-low, sons and daughters and grandsons and grand-daughters. Probably, the marriage of different individual brought to exist the institution of family.

With the passage of time, the early Meitei society came to transform in order to respond to the primary material needs of the community. The enlargement and development of the society were brought under the stress of certain conditions i.e. change of production activities, increase of population and absorption of immigrants. The gradual change of demographic structure resulted to prevail the disorder and difference among the descendent lineage groups of the ancient Meitei society. On the other hand, such circumstances led to extend even the boundary and also compelled the division of society into number of lineage groups.

Considerably, the Meitei kinship relation of lineage based society was dynamic in character and it became the key factor in the organization of social life of the Meiteis. The lineage was the fundamental unit of a social system which ultimately led to develop State society. Thereforc, in pristine Meitei society, lineage was considered as a basic social institution and it was formed by the union of the number of related kingships.

The clan society emancipated itself from immediate dependence on the caprices of raw nature. It was based on relatively simple technology using primary human and animal power. The clan community was partly self-sufficient but their production technique was primitive in many ways. Almost every individual was likely to engage in the production of food for consumption. Originally, land was protected by the chiefs for the clan people. Gradually, his protection was converted into theoretically ownership. In such situations, the producer no longer enjoyed the complete autonomy in his production because it was controlled to some extent by the ruling chief.

However, the increase of population and the development of settled agriculture compelled the clan people to reclaim more new lands for habitation and cultivation. L.H. Morgan states that:

> "presumptively when field agriculture demonstrated, the whole surface of the earth could be made the subject of property owned by individuals in severally and thus the new property career of mankind was inaugurated.[27]

In this stage, field agriculture in clan society by and large brought the system change of property ownership that unequal access to the means of production. However, wealth like land, grazing fields, fishing lakes, forests etc were unequally distributed. The difference of property owning resulted in stratifying the entire society.

There was no strict division of labour during the pre clan period. The pattern of division of labour was entirely based on sex and age. But the situation was changed during the clan period. It is fact that *numit kappa* (shooting of the sun) or Rebellion of slave against king an ancient Meitei literary work, records that in the Mangang clan there was stratification. It was not so complex but distinct peasant community including ruling class and slave existed. Possibly stratification is regarded as a precondition of Meitei state society.

Generally, it is reliable to highlight that natural location is one of the influencial factor to effect the early Meitei social formation, Robert Carneiro states that:

> "those regions in which areas are fertile land good land, should be surrounded by deserts or unproductive mountains or by the sea, when the population pressure results to increase competition and warfare in such region, the weaker or defeated or subjugated groups can not simply move away, as they typically do in regions where resources are loss differentiated when every rich land is tightly circumscribed, subordinated groups become absolutely tied down in their lower class or caste status."[28]

Certainly circumscription is one of the favourite reason to cause the early Meitei social formation. The valley of Manipur is naturally rounded by the mountain claims. The valley drained by numbers of smaller rivers, is highly fertile. And the number of the lake are found to scatter in different areas of valley. Both riverine and lake facilities are the common characteristic feature of it. Though, it lies in sub-tropical monsoon region, the climate is almost moderate around the year because of its natural location. Again its climate is probably monitered by its lakes. Since the dawn of prehistoric time, various ethnic tribes were attracted to this fertile valley. The process of diffusion and absorption of different ethnic groups are well documented which had finally formed into as many as seven clans. Early history of Manipur clearly indicates in its early sources that there existed more than seven clans and principalities. These clan people were tropical monsoon agriculturists living in permanent villages setting up their own separate smaller principalities fixed in definite boundaries governed by their respective chiefs. Although, they had different culture and ethnic identity, in brief, their occupation and food habit were almost similar. Since the absence of iron-curtain boundary, it was easy to move from one territory to another or from one pana to another. What matered was the loyalty of one individual or group to the chief of the particular *pana*.

Most probably, the aim of the migrants to Manipur valley was to search a new habitable land where abundant livelihood materials could be found or created. Those hordes of immigrants would be satisfied by the fertile riverine facility and warm climate of the valley. They definitely selected this valley region for their settlement. Their further migration would be largely restricted by the mountain barriers. Being induced by the availability of livelihood materials, they would not have will of further migration. In course of time, population of the valley, also increased under certain circumstances like migration and natural birth. Such instances brought to increase the number of population dependent upon agriculture. The eventual condition compelled the population to be a permanent force of competition and warfare. As the mountain ranges surround the valley of Manipur. They were unable to escape from the emerging happend. Therefore, the weaker or the defeated groups could not simply go away. In spite of settlement on the same altitude of same valley where resources are less differentiated, inter-clan contacts prevailed. Thus, the vanquished tribes were compulsorily amalgamated with the victorious groups. Ultimately it resulted to form super stratification which led to the emergence of unique Meitei social formation.

Nongda Lairen Pakhangba was owed to establish pristine Meitei State by conquest. The Meiteis under his able kingship probably distinguished themselves by building up a State society which was developed through its traditional socio-political and economic structures. Production activity i.e. the knowledge of cultivation was the prime reason to transform the valley dwellers from primitive simple society to a complex State society. However, the commencement of settle life resulted to exist property

However, the commencement of settle life resulted to exist property ownership class and the unequal access to the means of production emerged. The dissimilarity of property owning caused to stratify the entire Meitei society into two social classes like producer and enjoyer. The fopundation of early Meitei State followed the evolution of Meitei society for the first time in the annals of Manipur. Apart of production activities, pre-State existed social units were ever ready to respond the formation of distinct Meitei social structure. The early Meitei society was comprised of different grades such as ruling group, commoners and slaves.

Ruling Class

The concept of a king with absolute and divine powers is noteworthy to mention as an important mechanism of early social formations. Probably, the more centralized political structure brought development with the gradual extension of king Loiyumba's hegemony to the hill areas. Loiyumba's codification of law practically enriched tactful and wisdom measures resulted in which the recognition of the king as an absolute head of the State. His proclamation of the distribution of economic, administrative and social functions strengthened state's power which was weilded by people of various stratas and segments of the ruling class. These system entrenched to link between the lower social strata and ruler.

So far concern about particular heirarchical political structure of the Meitei kingdom, it can be stated that the *ningthou pongba tara* (ten chieftain) should be conceptualized in regional terms like *nongpok* (east), *chingkhei* (North-east), *wangpurel* and *khana chaoba* (both represents south), *thangjing* (South West), *sampurel, loyalakpa, kaobarel* (West), *kaoburel* and *marjing* (both represent North).[29] Besides, Meitei social formation further recongnized more heirarchical structures in the ruling group. These stratification were picked out as departmental post, clan chief and 64 *phamdous* (ministers). Hence, the functional and territorial implications would be the prime reason to make a water-tied compartment of ruling strata of the Meitei kingdom. The situation primarily served to fulfil the absolute power of the king.

The ruling class consisted of royal family and nobility (ten regional chieftain, 64 *phamdous* officials or ministers, clan chiefs and local chiefs or heads) who received the grants of land at the pleasure of the king. Brahmans also appeared as a separate strata. These officials headed all departments of the State. Except the chiefs of the clan, all the posts of the nobility were not hereditary. Generally, social mobility within the entire ruling class was fairly exercised. The Meitei kings were regularly favoured with addition to their harem of attractive daughters given to them by chieftains and higher functionaries. The new concubine's father was given gifts and lands. Undoubtedly, the sons of the king and concubines formed a nobility. In such way, a particular social status groups were formed. The lower stratum of the ruling class consisted of State functionaries who were lesser chiefs or heads who were responsible for mobilizing the *lallup* labours for war and public welfare works.

Commoners

The commoners comprised of peasant cultivators, various manual workers, priest etc. formed the material foundation of the early Meitei society. To a great extend, *lallup* service rendered to the State, was utilized in different construction works and repairing of roads and bridges, religious works, hydromanagerial and other welfare works. The water works provided a considerable extend of productive forces of the rice cultivators. It is reliable to mention that the controlling of *lallup* service developed the prime relation between the ruling class and the means of production. The *lallup* labour even appropiated non-productive works. Occasionally, craft-producers were instructed to perform specialist works. Thus, the State also entered to correspond or control village craft production. This situation indicates a clear cut existence of craft specialists social strata and development of separate social relation between the king and craft specialists and village craft specialists (i.e. Thongjao, Chairel, Khurkhul, etc.).

By introducing *lallup* system, King Loiyumba was successful to organize unpaid labour. King's ability to accomulate labour without spending a single coin could consolidate the centralized apparatus of the royal power. As all the able-bodied male section were obliged to cultivate one *pari* (two and half acre) of land, more reclamation of cultivable area began to expand. However, the pristine Meitei kingdom no longer faced the acute scarcity of labour. The new trend of structural transformation and improvement particularly socio-economic aspects exemplified that the Meitei society was no more stagnant. Possibly full scale development of social stratification signified the maturation of Meitei society, distinctively appeared during the kingship of Meidingu Loiyumba.

Slave

No doubt, the slaves were the main source of free or forced labour. Essentially most of the products made by them only benefited kings or nobles. The slaves were the lowest social stratum of the Meitei social formation. Since the slaves were the contributors to the State, any social relation between the slave and the State did apparently develop. However, their contribution have often been not recognised duly.

Since the dawn of the society, the Meiteis grew various kind of vegetables and fruits for their own use. Though the agriculture and fishing were considered most important occupation, every peasant household also grew fruits and vegetables for their own use. The important fruits and vegetables planted by the peasant agriculturists are sugarcane, betel, cotton, maize, tobacco, water melon, pineapple, sesame, jackfruit, pomegranate, guava, ginger, turmeric, mustard, brinjal, pumpkin, gourd, different kinds of beans, small onion, arum, sweet arum, cucumber,. etc. In addition to these, there were number of wild fruits and vegetables. These were largely grown for home use; but some excess of any product was bartered locally for another item. The primitive form of occupation like food gathering still continued. The wild collected fruits from the nearby forest and wild vegetables gathering from the marshes, lakes and forest would subsist their requirement. Furthermore, the peasant agriculturists not only collected house building materials like wood, cane, thatch grass i.e *tumnou*, *humdang, kangbong* but also acquired bamboo from surrounding homestead land, orchard and forest. Bamboo was used in different ways such as home making, tool making, making of house hold materials and vegetable.

Traditionally, craft production and other productive occupation played an important role in the development of economic situation of early Manipur. These are separately considered under the following ways:

Fishing

Definitely, fishing one of the earliest forms of the occupation of the valley dwellers was the second in importance to live in the economic life of the early Meiteis. Virtually, rivers, number of the lakes and streams found scattered in the valley provided a good fishing ground. Every household of the kingdom, used to catch plenty of fish during the flood season mainly for home consumption. But the villagers inhabited around the lakes caught fish regularly. Usually fishing was successfully done with the help of many shorts of nets, long (spike made of bamboo), line-hook (made of thread and hook), short hook (made of reed and hook) different types of *tyjeplu* (rectangular type made of cane and bamboo), *kaboru, tungoru, showaru* (made of bamboo piece) *long* (made of bamboo piece), *khoya* (made of thread and bamboo piece). The use of trunk boat faciliated the fishermen to catch the fish in different method.

Pottery

Pottery making is also one of the oldest occupation of the people of the kingdom of Manipur. Archaeologists clearly prove that pottery making was practised in Manipur since the neolithic period. About fortytwo tripod legs handmade potsherds both of plain and cordmarks with reddish brown colours were unearthed from Napachik hillock, a neolithic village situated at Wangoo of Bishnupur district.[29] During the historical period in Manipur, there were some pottery specialist villages such as Thongjao, Chairen, Andro, Sekta, Nungbi Tangkhul, Nongpok Sekmai etc. Different types of big and small potteries for various purposes were used by each and every household of Manipur. These developed as specialist villages in pottery making much later possibly during the medieval period.

Weaving

During the pre-Pakhangba period, even the people were acquainted of weaving, spinning and dyeing cotton clothes. Primarily, these works were done by the women. Usually cotton plant had been grown on the peasant's own premises but dyes always seemed to have been made from natural plant ingredients. Thus weaving and printing designs of female clothes were developed during the reign of Khuyai Tompok. It is also believe that silk manufacturing and its weaving for the first time started to practise during his reign *kabrang phanek* (female skirt made of silk) was weaved during the kingship of Naothingkhong.[30] In later period, the silk culture in Manipur was entirely in the hands of the *loi* villages. Considerably in the beginning both cotton clothes and silk clothes were weaved to the loen loom by the women. With the innovation of elaborate coronation customes known as Naothingkhong Phijet, however, the State authority entered to control weaving craft production. During the reign of Loiyumba, State had to regulate the organization of weaving industry under a definite law. King not only assigned 30 families to weave clothes and eight families were also fixed to introduce different colours.[31] Thus, the feudalization to weave craft was also for the first time recorded. The State's control over the weavers and dyers resulted in developing kingdom's economy.

Basket

Various types of baskets made of bamboo and stripes of cane were used in each and every household. Before the use of weight and measurement was not known to the early people of Manipur. The smaller, medium and bigger baskets were used as a measurement device. Since rice was a medium of exchange in early Meitei society, different types of baskets like *meruk, utong, masung, laitang, likhai* and *sangbai* were used. Baskets like Ngairuk, Ngarubak, Tungol were also made to keep fish. Besides baskets like *tabu* or *phirubak* were also manufactured for keeping clothes. These baskets were made specially by the elders in every lanes of villages in order to meet the household requirements. It was meant for community consumption.

Animal Husbandry

Before the commencement of agrarian structure, animal husbandry or cattle rearing was also an important occupation of the early people of Manipur. With the introduction of field agriculture, cattle rearing was continued to be practised widely. *numit kappa* (shooting sun) literary text mentions the domestication of horse. It is also reported that domestication of cow was known to the proto Meiteis. The domestication of various animals namely buffalo, cow, pig, horse, dog, cock, hen etc. benefited to ploughing, sacrificial food, war and transportation purposes.

Yu (country spirit) was also widely manufactured for drinking and ritual purposes. In spite of the distribution of certain natural resources in definite villages, specialised villages in particular occupations emerged. The iron deposit located at the bed of small streams south of Thoubal and hill near Langathel and thus blacksmith industry in Kakching village near these iron-ore producing area, was done. Salt wells were found at Chandrakhong, Ningel, Waikhong, Sikhong areas. Salt manufacturing works were done in the aforesaid villages under the care of *thumjaorungba* (Minister in-charge of salt).[32] Carpentary, jewellery, tool making, brick-making etc. were another important works done by the individual specialists.

Lallup Labour Production

Peasants' *lallup* service to the State was mainly used in digging of canals and ponds, dredging rivers, diversion of river courses, construction of roads, bridges and other welfare works. With the institutionalization of *lallup* service during the reign of Loiyumba brought to make adequate supply of worker for public works. The distribution of occupation to different lineage in the village commodity production of artistic works is attributed to the tendency of the ruling class to exploit the artisan skills of the peasantry through the diversion of lallup service owed to the State for welfare works. Inasmuch such systematic organization of peasant labour contributed to the expansion of productive forces of peasant rice cultivators. Usually products made by slave labour were made at the direction of the nobles and the king for their enjoyment. Forced labour was supplied by imprisoned criminals, debted persons, prisoner of war etc. King utilized slave labour in agriculture, cutting of firewood and tree, collecting vegetables, looking after kings' fishing lakes etc.

Market

During the early period, in Manipur also barter system the earliest mode of the medium of trade exchange was commonly performed for buying and selling purposes. The issue of bell metal coin by Ura Konthouba in his name marked the commencement of moneytization of the barter economy of the kingdom of Manipur. In 1614, Godly king Khagemba set up ten markets namely Sana Keithel, Moirang Keithel, Khuman Keithel, Phaibung Keithel, Chairen Keithel, Namphon (Nambol) Keithel, Kongnang Keithel and Andro Keithel(market). He also issued bell metal currency. These developments indicated the growth of mercantile society as well as moneytization of economy which faciliated the buying and selling of various commodities. Thus, the kingdom marked entery to a new phase of economic prosperity.[33]

Tax

The main sources of the tax as collected in the early Manipur were the war booty, tribute, *lallup* service, various food grains. Both Ningthourol Lambuba and Cheitharol Kumbaba mention about frequent feud between the Meitei kings and the Luwang, the Khuman and the Moirang principalities. Besides Meitei kings waged successive battles against the tribes and, the Shan principalities of Kabaw valley and even against the Burmese. Usually, the Meitei kings collected war booty from the defeated groups. They also received tributes from those subjugated tribes communities, principalities and kingdoms. *Lallup* service was another important form of tax which was rendered to the State. Land tax was the most important tax received by the State in kind. The State collected forest product from the forests and fishes from the lakes as State revenue. The kingdom was successfully governed with the assistance of these various sources of revenue collected at different levels in the State.

Patterns of Land-use

With the beginning of settled life, lands were too essential for the people who engaged in food gathering, hunting cultivation etc. The proto-Meiteis or the early people used to fight among themselves in order to acquire lands and other cattle wealth. However, the idea of land ownership came to birth soon after the development of agrarian structure. During the pre-State and early State society, it seems to develop some land ownership system which included crown land, communal land and private land and their ownership aspects.

Naothingkhong Phambal Kaba mentions that the king or chief of the clan principalities were the real owners of their respective territorial boundaries. King Naothingkhong acquired a large track of land after conquering the Haokei tribe. The arable land received by the king after defeating other tribes would be treated as the crown land. These crown lands were tilled by the slaves or through the lallup system.[34]

To a greater extent, by organizing human-labour, the Meitei kings reclaimed more cultivable lands. The village communities also would have reclaimed cultivable areas. Out of these aforesaid areas, some areas were demarcated as communal land. Besides, pastureground, fishing lake and forest areas were also reserved. The villagers worked together in the communal land areas and they enjoyed the products got from these areas collectively.

During the early period in Manipur, private ownership of land came to emerge on account of land grants. All the nobles were granted some portion of cultivable lands by the kings. Loiyumba Shinyel clearly points out that land grants were made to the war heros who got victory seven times in the war. Those brave hunters who captured tigers was given one pari of cultivable land." There are definite traditions that if a tiger was captured by seven persons, only three persons were granted lands.[35]

In the later period, the land owning system was developed extensively. The land owning system can be divided into

(1) King's cultivable land,

(2) *Phamlou* (official cultivable land),

(3) *Siphai lou* (Sepoy's cultivable land),

(4) *Mana lou* (rewarded areable land),

(5) *Brahmin lou* (rice land of the Brahmin),

(6) *Lairou* (cultivable land of the temple or forest gods), etc.[36]

It was started from the time of king Khagemba that the records of the land right were prepared under the department of revenue known as Lourungpural. *Loukok eba* (land record officer) arranged all the land records. There was an officer named *lourungba* (Chief recorder of land).[37] Another officer *phunan salungba's* duty was to supervise all matters connected with rice cultivation. He was responsible to look after the measurement, collected rent in kind and transacted all business matters connected with land on behalf of the king.[38] These officers of the State were highly respected by the people at large.

Since land belonged to the State, cultivators were to pay as a tax of areable land rent to the State. The land tax paid to the State varied from two baskets to thirteen from each *puree* (two and half acres). In later period, *sel* (cash) was also allowed to be paid as pay tax in lieu of paddy. Thus the Meitei kings systematically prepared the land tenure and properly generated land revenue which largely benefited in running the kingdom.

REFERENCES

1. R.B. Pemberton, *The Eastern Frontier of India* (Rep), New Delhi, 2000, p. 29.

2. O.K. Singh, *Archaeology in Manipur Series*, 1983, Imphal, pp. 1-3.

3. *Report of the Archaeology* Department Government of Manipur, Imphal, 1983, p. 5.
4. *Op. cit.*, pp .6-7.
5. N. Ibochouba Singh (Transcribe), *Third Layat*, Imphal, 1981, p. 5.
6. N. Ibochouba Singh (Transcribe), *Sakok Lamlen*, Imphal, 1981, p. 2.
7. N. Angou Luwang (Transliterate), *Kangbalon,* Imphal, 1976, pp. 1-2.
8. *Op. cit.*, pp. 1-3.
9. O. Bhogeshor Singh (Transcribe), *Numit Kappa*, Imphal,1977, pp. 1-2 & 28.
10. N. Angou Luwang, *op. cit.*, pp. 11-15 and O.Bhogeshor Singh, *Ningthourol Sheireng*, Imphal, 1967, pp. 95-102.
11. M. Chandra Singh (Transliterate), *Poireiton Khunthok*, Imphal, 1979, pp. 9-11.
12. N. Manouyaima Singh (Transcribe), *Tutenglon*, Kakching, pp. 16-17.
13. O. Bhogeshor Singh, *Ningthourol Lambuba*, Imphal, 1967, p. 37.
14. Gangmumei Kabui, *History of Manipur*, Vol.I, Pre-Colonial Period, New Delhi, 1991, pp. 219-220.
15. R. Brown, *Statistical Account of Manipur* (Rept.), New Delhi, 2001, p. 17.
16. Naorem Lokendra Singh (ed), *Land Use System in Manipur Hills*, New Delhi, 2004, p. 3.
17. R. Brown, *op. cit.*, pp. 85-86.
18. T.C. Hodson, *The Meitheis* (Rept.), Delhi, 1989, p. 40.
19. E.N. Dun, *Gazetteer of Manipur*, London, 1886, p. 60.
20. *Ibid.*, pp. 99-100.
21. R. Brown, *op. cit.*, p. 88.
22. Khulem Chandrashekhar Singh, *Loiyumba Shinyen*, Imphal, 1975, pp. 17-18 & 20-23.
23. Gangmumei Kabui, *op. cit.*, p. 129.

24. *Ibid.*, pp. 199-200.
25. Wahengbam Ibohal Singh, *The History of Manipur* (An Early Period), Imphal, 1986, p. 608.
26. L.H. Morgan, *Ancient Society*, New Delhi (Rept), 1968, pp. 553-4.
27. R. Cohen and E.R. Service, *The Anthropological Political Evolution*, 1978, Philadelphia, p. 28.
28. N. Ibobi Singh, *Manipur Administration from 1709-1909*, Imphal, 1982, p. 24.
29. O. Kumar Singh, *Archaeology in Manipur*, Imphal, p. 22.
30. Ch. Manihar Singh (translated), *Naothingkhong Phambal Kaba*, Imphal, 1982, p. 32.
31. Gangmumei Kabui, *op. cit.*, p. 220.
32. T.C. Hodson, *The Meitheis* (Rept.), Delhi, 1997, p. 31.
33. Gangmumei Kabui, *op. cit.*, pp. 106-220.
34. M. Narendra Singh (trnscribe), *Khongchamnupi Nongkarol*, Imphal, 1967, p. 33.
35. Kh. Chandrashekhar Singh, *op.cit.*, p. 16.
36. R. Brown, *op. cit.*, pp.85-6; W. Yumjao Singh, *Report on Archaeological Studies in Manipur*, Buletin Chapter II, Appendix IV, P. 1 and L. Ibungohal Singh, *Introduction to Manipur*, Imphal, 1963, p. 85.
37. Gangmumei Kabui, *op. cit.*, p. 218.
38. R. Brown, *op.cit.*, p. 86.

4

Typology of Hydraulic Management: Experience of Some Asiatic Kingdoms

A State came to emerge either through a long historical human epochs or conquests. Primarily, conflict is considered as an immediate reason for the birth of a State. However, the questions for survival and maintenance are matters of discussion for the newly established kingdom. On the one hand, the king is responsible for nurturing a State. Therefore, he launches various programmes and devices in order to effect the maintenance of the kingdom . It is believed that the king's hydraulic programme is one of the governing factors to attain stability as well as a State apparatus. A State is required to control the water bodies mainly through dredging rivers, digging canals, and ponds, supplying storing water and water to the agricultural fields etc. Such type of State is apparantely termed as hydraulic civilization or hydraulic society. Karl A. Wittfogel maintains that

> "the traditional designation of oriental society as synonimous for hydraulic society."[1]

It would have to be mentioned that there are two forms of hydraulic works such as non-agrarian hydraulic works and agrarian hydraulic works. Both aforesaid hydraulic works are the two dynamic common characteristic features of a hydraulic society.[2] Karl A.Wittfogel also classifies:

> "the hydraulic works into (A) Productive installations (canals, acquaducts reservoirs, sluices and dikes for the purpose of irrigation) and (B) Protective installations (Drainage canals and dikes) for flood control."[3]

He further classifies the non-agrarian hydraulic works rainfall farming, hydro agriculture and hydraulic agriculture. However, hydro agriculture based on small scale irrigation farming involves a intensity of cultivation on irrigated fields and often also non-irrigated fields. But it does not involve a division of labour on a communal, territorial or national level. On the other hand, hydraulic agriculture involves a specific type of division of labour. It intensifies cultivation. And it necessiates cooperation on a large scale.[4]

In rainfall farming region, there is practically absence of labour and the farmers themselves manage water supplied by rain by using their traditional local techniques. According to different topographical location of various civilization, the pattern of hydromanagerial programme are found uneven. According to E.Hunt and Robert C. Hunt:

> "there are many varieties of society practising irrigation and many forms of irrigation. Large water works to control major floods may differ greatly in their effect on society from filmsy water-works on small streams or from the building of one isolated qanal. A situation in which upstream irrigators can control water flow has to be quite different from one in which they cannot."[5]

It is required to highlight that a precise consideration for some of the South East Asian experience of hydraulic kingdoms including Funan (Combodia), Ahom, Thai or Tai and Manipur for better understanding is required. Typologically South East Asian States can be catagorised into maritime commercial kingdoms, land-based agricultural kingdoms and bureaucratic kingdoms. The birth of these different types of States highly depended on geo-political and economic factors. From time to time, king adopted multi-method secondary traits like relegious works, trade and commerce, collection of tributes, water managerial programmes etc. to make these States alive. Probably, the philosophical idea of employing these secondary traits were to gain massive loyalty of his subjects.

Funan (Combodia)

Ancient maritime commercial Funan kingdom was

established in present Cambodia sometime during the first or second century A.D. Perhaps, early Funan leaders capitalized on growing maritime trade from China to Middle East and Europe. Thus, Funan tended to grow rapidly as a maritime commercial kingdom. The ruling class would have acquired tax from the trading activities. No doubt, Funan was a group of allied ports.[6] It's port city Oc-Eo, of course, prospered due to serving as the terminus for the westward segment of the trade route leaving for China and the possession of a safe harbour.[7]

With great transformation of navigational skill from the primitive coastline or coastal trade to direct transoceanic trade brought a tremendous impact on Funan kingdom. It's coastal polity based on maritime trade, apparently collapsed and it was soon replaced by a land-based agricultural system. By and large Funan kingdom continued to expand through the 6th century A.D. At that time the centre of international trade was shifted from Oc-Eo to the Strait of Malacca. However, the loose of trade revenue compelled the leaders of the Funan to practise extensive agricultural work and further to expand its inland control of rice producing areas. It's society was stratified and her population engaged advanced method of water control and rice agriculture.[8] Since the attention paid more to wet rice cultivation in order to regenerate revenue, Funan also required to have increased its agricultural productivity by draining mangrove swamps and introducing irrigated agriculture. The innumerable channels faciliated water borne traffic and communication within the kingdom.[9] Thus, Funan controlled reverine plain of southern and central Combodia.

The availability of her natural channels and reverine facilities provided a great advantageous to evolve early Funan kingdom. Besides, the control of these water bodies and the investment of labour in irrigational canals to procure revenue would have made a perpitual device to bring the stability of the kingdom. Thoroughly the Funan Kingdom adopted the pattern of hydroagriculture based on irrigation farming. Thus, the kingdom paid more attention to the agrarian hydraulic works in its later phase. The transition of Funan society particularly easy because of the good agricultural hinterland not far from the Funan coast. "The 7th century Combodian epigraphic corpus clearly testifies to a society existing on rice agriculture in which the impetus to growth was perhaps based partly on wealthy traders moving inland chiefs who had already grown wealthy supplying trade goods in earlier times.[10]

Karl A.Wittfogel and his followers have characterized the prototypic irrigated society on the basis of their model of China and South East Asia. In such societies,the political life is controlled by an elitist bureaucracy of full time specialists both secular and religious powers.[11] No doubt, the later phase of Funan society can be coined as a hydraulic agricultural society due to full scale involvement in irrigated rice cultivation.

Manipur

The Meitei kings carried out the hydromanagerial works in the following processes:

(i) **Making of *Khong* or Canal:** The objectives of it were to drain innundated water from the swamps and marshy areas to create shoy or fishing weir, to supply water to the limited agricultural fields and to extend agricultural and habitational areas.

(ii) **Dredging and Diversion of Rivers:** The main purposes of it were to control flood and to make river transport facility.

(iii) **Building of *Thingel* or Dike:** The main intension of it was to control flood.But the villagers were erecting Thingels or dike across the streams to provide water to cultivable fields.

(iv) **Establishment of Reserved Fishing Ground in Different Parts of the Lakes:** The main objective of it was to collect fish as a revenue.

(v) **Construction of Public Ponds and *Thangapats* or Canal:** The first is to preserve drinking water. Second is used for defensive purpose.

The geo-physical knowledge of the Meitei king and their active responses to shape the surrounding environment became a notable integrative centralized character of the State. The frequent and continous participation of the masses in the public works like religious and secular works enhanced the sense of integration, loyalty and responsibility and these assertiveness contributed by the people were the substential reason to strengthen the development of the State.

Karl A. Wittfogel modifies his prototypic hydraulic society because some of the conditions of his ideal model can not be met by the scale of society and the scale of the irrigation. Probably, the special elements of the hydraulic are a single physical irrigation system, massive in scale managed by highly centralized despotic regim.[12] But, he further classifies the hydraulic system into hydroagriculture and hydraulic-agriculture according to the degree and standard water management programme of a society. Though the primary Meitei State cannot be termed as real hydraulic agricultural society, nevertheless it can attain the level of hydro agricultural society as well as rainfall farming. The available records clearly show that the Meitei kings practically carried out more non-agrarian massive hydromanagerial works than the agrarian hydraulic works.

Ahom Kingdom

Tai-Ahom State was established in 1228 by Hso-ka-Hpa, the first Ahom king by conquest.[13] Historical events prove that the Ahom State was secondary in nature. They introduced various means like subjugation, absorption, wet rice cultivation and Shakta Hinduism, to make Ahom kingdom a full-fledged State.

Wet rice irrigated cultivation was one of the possible factor controlled by the Ahom kings to run the State effectively is discussed. Amalendu Guha makes a detail survey of the Tai-Ahom political development and the practice of wet-rice cultivation backed by the irrigation. When studies the secondary Tai-Ahom State, Guha mainly emphasises on its socio-political evolution of them. The early phase of the Tai-Ahom State formation was considered as Tribalism by Guha. According to him, "the rudementary Ahom State based on many agricultural village (ban) settlement, each made up of a certain number of big or small families belonging to different family groups (foil). Number of such settlements combined together and formed an intermediate unit or domain with one of the village settlements as the headquaters of the noblemen governing it. At the apex of the several domains, there was a king including his colleagues like nobles and officers appointed by him."[14]

Guha also highlights the transformation of economic structure with the establishment of the Tai-Ahom State. They introduced *sali* (wet rice cultivation) cultivation to the subdued Morans and Bohari tribes who produced *chu* rice with slash and burn methods. However, an extensive river valley area was brought under sali cultivation which is high yield crop. This enabled them to possess surplus production helped largely to develop the kingdom in full swing. He also, thus, States that

> "statehood emerges only when a community produces a surplus sufficient for the maintenance of a non-producing public authority."[15]

In such way, the Tai-Ahoms certainly became superior to those neighbour kingdoms like the Kacharies and the Chutias. He points out that the Ahom king's attention to build up large-scale embarkment served as bund to restrict the heavy innundation which was also used as road. Besides, the embankment digging areas was filled up with water brought by inundation and rain. This water was utilised for the field agriculture. Such programme of construction provided great advantage to carry out successfully wet-rice culture in Upper Assam.[16] For heavy construction embankment work required large number of workers. In this respect, king organized manpower by financing and using his power. Thus king centralized his power and made it effective in State apparatus.

R. Buragohain exactly applies Karl A Wittfogel's idea of hydraulic society to the Tai Ahom society. He pleads that:

> "ecologically the Tai-Ahom State had to be a hydraulic State."

However, the Ahom kings took a great initiation to construct embankments and dykes to restrict flood from the heavy inundation of the parenial Brahmaputra and its tributaries. For such constructions, the Ahom king organized labour and manpower. His organization programme of manpower strengthened the king's centralization power which effected the development of State. On the other hand, the dykes and embankments were used as irrigational canals for sali paddy cultivation provided the infrastructure in the society which is highly co-related to the State apparatus. These developments gave rise to agro-managerial despotism.[17]

Tai Kingdom

In A.D. 1238, the paternalistic Sukhothai kingdom was founded by Sri Intratit by conquest. Traditionally Tais are wet-rice agriculturists. Since the kingdom was situated in intermountain basin, the cultivation was primarily performed through distributary system of water management. Such system brought to prevail a complex system of social relation among the fellow farmers.[18] It is realised that in this stage, a single family enjoyed a free holdership of the land and they cultivated in their own fields according to their ability. Agriculture developed the system of direct co-operation among the fellow farmers (i.e. it was seen at the time of harvesting). On the other hand, the practice of agriculture in wide scale by the Sukhothai people resulted in producing surplus food mostly consumed by its own people and agriculture became an important factor to exist Sukhothai society as a material foundation society.[19]

According to the geographical variation and with the development and expansion of the Tai world, they performed swidding or upland dry-rice cultivation, low and wet-rice cultivation with broad casting and transplantation.[20] The Tais performed swidding cultivation when they were in their homeland region and in the northern frinze of Angkor Empire. With the commencement of their second civilization in the northern part of the Chao Phraya valley particularly in Sukhothai region, they developed the system of low land wet-rice cultivation. However, the full-swing expansion of Tai civilisation probably followed the wet-rice cultivation by transplantation. After the foundation of first Tai kingdom of Sukhothai by conquest, the key factor of State development was the stability of population created by successful agriculture operated with the help of irrigation and other works.

The magnificent success of the Tais installation of a State at Sukhothai was the unquestionable example of the possession of population, territory, government, ruler etc. Thus, the Tai ruler of Sukhothai in order to gain legitimacy of power and the centralisation of power, required to control population by means of increasing surplus production in society. It resulted in developing material foundation society characterized by classes and caste.

E. Hunt believes that:

> "there is a clear relation between water control and the source of power of the ruling elites of the irrigated society. But it is essential to remain that there are many varieties of society practising irrigation and many forms of irrigation that either in large or small scale. On the otherhand the elite bureaucracy also undertook other massive water works by repairing and digging canals. Considerably the ruling bureaucracy builds (navigation canal and irrigation canals) and reinforces its power because it can effectively carry out the functions and roles required to be managed by the masses."[21]

It is found to record in the stone inscription of Sukhothai that:

> "irrigation was practised in this period. It further recorded that the king constructed an irrigation canal from Son Gve all the way to Sukhothai. It provided water both to upland and lowland forms and people planted area palms and caught fish."[22]

The Sukhothai population was divided into two classes i.e. Chao or ruling class headed by the king and the commoners.[23] The commoners were the source of manpower. The people were to render the compulsory State services and they were to some as an army during the war time. And they were obliged to work for the State at the time of peace.

The establishment of powerful Tai kingdom over the central part of the Chao Phraya plain brought tremendous advantages in the field of agriculture. It is recorded in the *Anals of Ayudhya* (particularly the period of Ramatibodi II) that in A.D. 1498 two ancient canals were repaired by deepening and clearing. It also mentions that in A.D. 1510 restoration of irrigation of an irrigation canal among other royal works was carried out. Thus, the Ayuthian kings carried out irrigation work by improving existing ones.[24]

In many sphere, Ayudhya was more advanced than Sukhothai. While Ayudhya is situated on three rivers coverage of rich alluvial valley. Sukhothai stands along the shore of a smaller river.[25] However, the Tai became an abundant rice producer by performing wet rice cultivation with the help of monsoon rain which was brought to field through irrigation canals and inundation of river water feed by rain. Population came to increase by attracting immigrants and war captives brought by the Ayudhian rulers. Therefore, large cultivable areas were reclaimed.

The establishment of Tai capital in Bengkok followed the expansion of settlement, the further encouragement of the reclamation of the cultivable areas and the introduction of plantation agriculture. However, large scale plantation agriculture began smoothly with the help of canal water and largely with the assistance of the river as well as rain water. Hence, sufficient amount of agricultural yield was furtherly reported. It shows the expansion of cultivable areas over the Chao Phraya valley and production increased. During the reign of Narai the great, the permission was given to export rice.[26]

James C. Ingram estimates that in 1850, the population was almost wholly engaged in agriculture and rice was the principal crop. It was successfully cultivated over the Chao Phraya river valley which was flooded in every year with a fair degree of regularity. Thus, the rice production was enough to feed the people and after keeping for their annual consumption, rice was exported to solve the problem of failure of a rice crop in southern China.[27] Such increase in production proved that the Tai society was no more stagnated as Karl Mark states in his Asiatic Mode of Production that Asiatic Society is prolong stagnate.

According to Quaritch Wales:

> "during this Bangkok period, tens of thousands of acres of unproductive land were brought under cultivation with the help of irrigation."[28]

Dramatic development of agriculture took place during reign of Chulalongkorn by minimising or suspending the tax on rice field and implementing the irrigation projects, he promoted the extension of rice cultivation.[29]

In a paper entitled "An Ecological Interpretation of Thai History" Yoshikazu Takaya analyses the development and expansion of agricultural areas which was a factor to transform the Tai society in many ways. His elaborate discussion is briefly studied in order to fulfil the subject of argument (i.e. that Tai society was no more stagnated):

> "The first independent Sukhothai kingdom located on a mountain-embraced fan at the edge of the central plain of the Chao Praya. The kingdom enjoyed the apex of the distributary system of the intermountain basin. Probably here was treated as a central rice growing area of distributary system. On the other hand, such apex area became a focal point of the untralization of power. In the distributary system, a complex system of relation between the farmers of apex areas and the farmers of distributary areas came to exists. The apex farmer monopolised the water by building dams and canals. their main occupation was wet rice cultivation by broadcast. The shifting of the Tai centre from Sukhothai to Ayudhya faciliated the Tai to enjoy a vast cultivable flood plain of the Chao Phraya river. This plain is one to two hundred kilometres wide and about four hundred kilometres long. By and large, the Tais

performed wet-rice cultivation successfully over the vast area. The expansion of unprecedental cultivable area pushed up the annual yield several time than before. The Tai society in Ayudhya period apparently happened to develop and transform in many ways. The complex system of social relation between the producers and consumers came to emerge. Ayudhya's location on the bank of the Chao Phraya river witnessed the centre of commercial post. The establishment of the Tais capital at Bangkok on the strategic delta region of the Chao Praya river further expanded the reclamation of agricultural areas. The plantation agriculture, which enabled an increased production, was introduced in this delta region. However, its trade also reached maturity by improving the old canals and digging the new ones. The Tais was considerably found changing and developing in every stage of their shifting centre"[30]

According to D. Elliot, in central Thailand rice cultivation was successfully practised with the help of irrigation, rain water and inundation water of the river. Most water managerial and irrigation works in Chao Praya valley were done by social labour power (corvee labour) in the form of public works projects and the major canal networks and dams were constructed and managed by gangs of workers. In the northern part, there was upland soil condition minimum alluvium. The essential water of transplantation of rice cultivation was sufficiently provided by rainfall and numerous streams. He further states that nearly all irrigation work or means i.e.wires, dikes and small canals, were very simple and managed by the immediate users. However, the elite bureaucracy seems to have inactive to evolve the construction of irrigation projects and water managerial works but most of these works seem to be in the hands of the users or perhaps of community in some instances. The north-east region received scanty rainfall, therefore, upland methods of rice cultivation concentrated in small area having enough water to irrigate the fields. In the south, some upland form of rice cultivation was performed."[31]

As a whole it will not be appropriate to study the pre-capatalist

As a whole it will not be appropriate to study the pre-capatalist Tai economy within the framework of Asiatic Mode of Production avocated by Karl Marx. It is resolved that the pre-capatalist Tai social and economic patterns would not have exact counterpart in Marxian Asiatic Mode of Production. Therefore, there were general differences between the features of Tai despotism and the Asiatic despotism developed by Karl Marx.[32]

Marx states that irrigated way of cultivation was only one of the key aspects of the emergence of Asiatic despotism. His main emphasis is that the arid land of Asia could not be brought under cultivation in large scale without artificial irrigation works. Usually, the village community separately or in association could not undertake large scale irrigation works because of the vastness of territories and low level of civilization. But such work was carried out successfully by the government and it leads to the existence of the powerful and centralised Asiatic Despotism. So far concern about the typical features of Thailand, it can be put one by one for better understanding. In Thailand, there is vast cultivable river valley. Cultivation was widely practised throughout the kingdom successfully with the help monsoon rain water. Besides, some part of the central plain's cultivation was also done with the help of irrigation usually sponsored by the government. In Thailand, probably the centralization political apparatus was brought by both irrigation and navigational canal works which were responsible to rise of Tai despotism. The characteristic features of Asiatic despotism are to be found more typically in Asia are given below:

(1) The political state of the people does not exist, it is nothing but the private caprice of a single individual.

(2) The king was the proprietor of land and there was no any intermediary class like feudalism state or class check him.

(3) Slaves or slave owners did not exist in Asian society, all were general slaves below the despot.

The Siamese kings were not only initiation in the construction programme of irrigation canal projects but they were also highly conscious of the other water work programme like the establishment of navigational canals and digging wells to solve drinking water problem. It is fact that King Ramatibodi I dug wells to solve the scarcity of drinking water. By digging new canals such as the Simarong and the Tubnang canals and improvement of the existing ones, King Boromtrailokanat was responsible to faciliate internal water transport.[33] During the reign of King Prajairaja, a new canal Glon Pankok Hyai was dug out in order to make shorten the distance from the sea to Ayudhya.[34] King Taisra, by concription of 30,000 workers completed the digging of the Mahajai canal. However, Lawad canal was also constructed during the kingship of Taksin. King Rama I took a great initiation to dig a new canal to shorten the river transport.

It was during the reign of Rama III (1824-1850) at least four waterway projects were completed to construct including a canal thrity three miles long, built within two years.[35] King Mongkut also took up the plan of construction new canals in order to promote facility of the communication system between the capital and its adjoining towns. As far as possible large canal projects were undertaken by irrigation departments at the time of king Lhulalongkorn. Thus, by the end of 19th century in Thailand, there were several thousand kilometres of water ways regularly functioned.[36]

It is estimated that different hydraulic enterprises would attribute manifold results either directly or indirectly in Asiatic Tai society. The sociological significance of digging of wells, repairing or improving old ones and digging new canals particularly for the purposes of drinking water, irrigation and communication were to control manpower with legitimised central political power. The utilitarian work of waterways stimulated the flow of wealth into the royal treasury whereas the irrigation works would get some portion of production from the peasant agriculturist. None could gather manpower except the king because the control of such projects required capital and effective management power to organise the labours. In the context of Siam or Thailand, only the ruling elites were capaciated to carry out such enterprising programme. In exchange their manual subscription work, they considerably would enjoy royal protection and perhaps other benefits also. The corvee labour or commoners were compulsory obliged to render royal command in such public welfare works. To a greater extend, the Tai king would have got enormous success to organise manpower effected largely to State apparatus.

REFERENCES

1. Karl A.Wittfogel, *Oriental Despotism*, New Haven, Yale University Press, 1957 1st publication, p.8.
2. *Op. cit.*, p. 30.
3. *Op. cit.*, p. 42.
4. *Op. cit.*, pp. 22-23.
5. R. Cohen and E.R. Service, *Origin of State: The Anthropology of Political Evolution*, Philadelphia, 1979, p. 73.
6. Michael Vickery, Society, *Economy and Political in Pre- Angkor Combodia, The 17th-18th centuries, 1998*, The Toyo Bunko, Tokyo, p. 19.
7. Donald G. McCloud, *Southeast Asia Tradition and Modernity in the Contemporary World*, Westview Press Boulder, San Francisco, Oxford, p. 22.
8. Michael Vickery, *op. cit.*, pp. 19-20.
9. D.G.E. Hall, *A History of South East Asia*, London, 1955, p. 23.
10. Michael Vickery, *op. cit.*, pp. 325-26.
11. R. Cohen and E.R. Service, *Origin of State: The Anthropology of Political Evolution*, 1978, p. 70.
12. N. Manaoyaima Singh, *Tutenglon*, 1986, Kakching, pp. 2-5.
13. Saroj Nalini Arambam Paratt (Translated), *The Court Chronicle of the kings of Manipur, Routledge-Tylor and Francis Group*, London and New York, 270 Madison Ave-New York,2005, p. 23.
14. O. Bhogeshor Singh, *Ningthourol Sheireng*, Imphal,1987, pp. 221-22.
15. N. Angou Luwang, *Pakhangba Nongkarol* (trnscribe), Imphal, 1983, p. 27.

16. Gangmumei Kabui, *History of Manipur*, Vol.I Pre-Colonial Period, New Delhi, 1991, p. 219.
17. *Op. cit.*, pp. 227-28.
18. Ch. Manihar Singh (Translated), *Naothingkhong Phambal Kaba*, Imphal 1982, p. 21.
19. H. Nilkant Singh, *Early Political System of Manipur and Thailand*, Imphal, 2006, p. 26.
20. R. Cohen and E.R. Service, *op. cit.*, p. 70.
21. P. Gogoi, *The Tai and the Tai kingdom in Assam*, Gauhati University, Gauhati, 1968, p. 251.
22. Amolendu Guha, *Medieval and Early Colonial Assam, Society, Polity, Economy*, New Delhi, 1991, p. 82.
23. *Ibid.*, pp. 67, 70 and 71.
24. *Ibid*, p. 74.
25. *Proceedings of North East India History Association*, Fifth Session, Aizawl, 1984, p. 45.
26. *Journal of South East Asian Studies*: Vol.VI No.2, September, 1975, University of Singapore, pp. 192-193.
27. David Elliot, *Thailand: Origin of Military Rule*, London, 1979, p. 33.
28. *Ibid*, p. 27.
29. R. Cohen and E.R. Service, *op. cit.*, pp. 72-73.
30. D.Elliot, *op. cit.*, p. 36.
31. D.K.Wzatt, *Thailand: A Short History*, New Haven, 1984, p. 58.
32. H.G.Quaritch Wales, *Ancient Siamese Government and Administration*, New York, 1965 (Rept.), p. 230.
33. D. Elliot, *op. cit.*, p. 34.
34. Rong Syamananda, *History of Thailand*, Bangkok, 1981, p. 72.
35. James C.Ingram, *Economic Change in Thailand 1850-1970*, Standford, 1971, p. 8.
36. Quaritch Wales, *op. cit.*, p. 230.
37. Rong Syamanda, *op. cit.*, p. 130.

38. *Journal of Southeast Asian Studies,* Vol. VI No. 2 September, 1975, p. 69.
39. D. Elliot, *op. cit.,* pp. 41, 60-63.
40. Bipan Chandra, *Karl Marx, His Theories of Asian Societies and Colonial Rule,* New Delhi, p. 11.
41. Rong Syamanda, *op. cit.,* p. 41.
42. Quaritch Wales, *op. cit.,* p. 230.
43. W.V. Steffin, *The Thai Bureaucracy,* Institutional Change Development, Honolulu, 1960, p. 16.
44. Rong Syamananda, *op. cit.,* p. 46.

5

Cultural Importance of Water Work

Early settlers of Manipur were widely benefited by nature. They selected the water body areas. These were their habitational ground in order to get transportation, daily using of water, fishing and gathering facilities. Consequently, the Meitei paid respect to the water deities and rain gods. They worshipped properly these deities with elaborate rituals in order to get save from draught and flood. The religious belief system must have developed later.

According to the Meitei concept of "Leishemba" in creation of the Earth, water is one of the component part of it. For the maintenance and regulation of water, various female and male deities were assigned according to different seasons. So far as concern about the water body the Meiteis used to believe that water body had been divided into three major respective layers i.e. upper layer, middle layer and under water. The upper layer of water was put under the control of *eraleima* (Female deity) while the middle layer was assigned to *ekheileima* (Female deity). The last under water layer belonged to *ereima* (female deity). Besides these foresaid female deities, there were other male water deities like *eram-maba tumaba* (controller of stream or channel), *eram semba tusemba* (manager of canal) and *kum sana kumliklai* (messenger of water that whether water of a year will be plenty or not). When the rainy season is in the offing, new water is flown down to the rivers, streams, lakes, canals, ponds etc. During the rainy season, these female water deities were worshipped with presentation of *Cheng, Lei, Uhei-Wahei* (rice, flower, fruits) after reciting some hymns. Probably, it was the prayer of seeking permission by the people to use water for the new coming year. The dwelling of Erammaba Tumaba and Eramsemaba Tusemba in the canals and streams reflected to the minds of each and every people of Manipur that individuals should not make dirty and block these. It was also believe that whenever any person committed mistake against the customary norms, he was awarded of illness. Hence, the people were compelled to accept proper maintenance and safeguard of the water bodies. The Meitei termed water bodies as *pat* (lake), *turel* (river), *eram* (stream or channel), *khong* (canal), *pukhri* (pond), *loukhong* (irrigated canal), *khongban* (smaller canal surrounding courtyard of house). According to the availability of water in various place, early people of Manipur named it differently. These are *tu* (water of stream), *tarang* (flood water of vast area), *laicha* (water of Loktak), *yingou* (river water), *yimu* (Lake water), *yiriba lai* (inundated water to the low lying areas) and *yishing*(water).[1]

Pumshai khong located inside the Kangla was the source of other three important branches of canals like Khakhong, Laikhong and Marakhong. These water shed points were ever associated with the myth and the beliefs of the Meiteis. The Meiteis worshipped Khakhong for wealth and prosperity. Marakhong was also venerated with an elaborate ritual work for the richness, promotion etc. The belief in the worship of Laikhong was to give life. Laikhong is believed as an originating place of eight *umanglai*(forest gods) namely Muwakol, Chakhakol, Mongbakol, Yumoikol, Taothingkol, Yoiheikol, Naokhangkol and Tinshikol. Such instances certainly highlight that the gods were supposed to dwell in these canals controlled and possessed by the Meitei rulers and their ancestors. The ever association of the Meitei kings to the mythical water points or sources symbolised power, respect and awesome, loyalty, etc.[2]

On the other hand, there were number of regional gods who controlled rain. They were Thangjing, Koubru, Loyarakpa and Kounu. Usually the Meiteis believed in *kumdamba* (kum= year and damba=forecaster of rainy season of a year). According to the situation of cloud and direction of the wind, Kumdamba was assigned to one of the aforesaid gods. Thus, the Meiteis particularly scholars of palace declared the *kumdamba lai* (forecaster) of rain for one year. If the rain came from the Thangjing range direction, Manipur received enormous rain and then the *thangjing lai* (god) was proclaimed as a *kumdamba/ kumkhaiba* (forecaster) of that year. Scientifically, south-west monsoon blows from the Bay of the Bengal enters Manipur from Thangjing range side. But if the *kumdamba* was done by Koubru, in that year Manipur would enjoy medium of rainfall. It is reported that if *kounu lai* (god) acted as *Kumdamba*, Manipur got rain very scarcely. If *Kumdamba* was carried out by *Loyarakpa* (god), Manipur faced drought. When the rain was either scarce or absent, the Meiteis used to perform *Nong Kouba* (Nong = rain and kouba = call) ritual work. Such *Nong Kouba* ritual work was done in different ways. One of *Nong Kouba* was effected by some of the particular villages; second type was executed by the king or nobles; and the third type of *Nong Kouba* was operated mainly by the women folk of *Khwairamband Keithel*. The basic object of carrying out such a ritual work was to bring rain down to the earth by offering different edable things, reciting hymns and singing song *Nongnao Eshei* (song of rain). *Wangparel Khana Chaoba* (regional god), resided in the southern part of the Manipur valley supervised the river run towards the south. Seasonally, he was worshipped not only to inflict harm on the people but also to provide plenty of fish.Such were the Meitei belief.

In Manipur, there were more than sixty lakes during the early periods. It is believed that different gods had owned these Lakes respectively. Hence, there was customary to worship these gods at least once in a year according to convenience. The best example is that Thangjing was venerated for the Loktak Lake because he owned the lake. For Lamphel *pat* (lake), *Luwang Pokpa* (Proginator of Luwang) was adorned. Some of the other important lakes were put under the authorityship of clan progenitors like *Khuman Pokpa* (Progenitor of Khuman) managed Pumlel *pat* (lake), *Chenglei Pokpa* (Progenitor of

Chenglei) supervised Takyel *pat* (lake), *Angom Pokpa* operated Kongpa Mairompa Nganpa owned Teknkha *pat* (lake) Khapa looked after Ikop lake, Hairem Khunchan controlled lake located between Kiriching Chinglak and Yirong *pat* (lake) belonged to Wurok Wushai Sarang Leishangthem maintained Loitang lake.[3]

When the clan people prayed their *apokpa* (progenitor) they certainly collected water from different lakes and ponds where their clan progenitor seemed to dwell. The system clearly indicates the virtual socio-economic and political relationship between the clan people and lakes. Besides these, king initiated to perform different forms of worship regarding water management works. Usually an elaborate ritual work was undertaken before digging ponds, canals and riverbeds and construction of dikes and *shoy* (fishing weir). After finishing of digging and construction of these an inauguration ceremony with rituals were possibly performed. Even for the protection of dykes, ritual ceremony was performed.

Water is an integral part of the Meitei civilization. The controlling of water body systems enhanced the power of the kings. The Meiteis used to believe that some of the important canals and lakes were ever associated with the creation of the earth. In order to generate their power and to make ever embody with the water-shed systems, water from specific three canals (most probably from Khakhong, Laikhong and Marakhong) was taken and it was utilized for bathing the king at the time of his coronation ceremony with elaborate hymns. The glaring example is that before ascending the throne, a coronation ceremony was performed. In such ceremony, *ningthou pongba tara* the ten regional chieftain and the chief advisors of the king collected water from the *eram* (streams) and rivers. By using these specific water, King Naothingkhong was given bath with elaborate hymns.[4] The hymns are given below in varnacular Manipuri language:

Manipuri version	*English Translation*
"Koupa kounu yi,	Water collected from the stream which rises from the Kouba Kounu peak of Koubru hill
Yireng Yikhamyi,	Water collected from the stream flows to the Yireng Yekham area
Chingbal Charlyi,	Water collected from the stream flows to the Chingbal Charl area
Chenglei Luwang Luwangyi,	Water collected from Chenglei owned portion of Luwangyi river
Singtha Leithom Yi,	Water collected from the stream runs to the area of Singtha Leithom area
Takna Leirongyi,	Water collected from the stream runs to the area of Takna Leirong area
Kapong Nawangyi	Water collected from the stream flows to the area of Kapong Nawangyi area Asangpam Leima Waikoiyi
Arampam Waychatyee,	Water collected from the stream runs through the settlement areas of Asangpam and Arampam lineages
Kongpa Yeerik Laysengyi,	Water collected from the Kongba river
Thayong Sumpa Lokchaoyi,	Water collected from Lokchao of Thayong Sumpa area
Chengkoy Narlyi,	Water collected from Chengkoy Narlyi river.
Mamai Awang Laina Pangna Chenpayi,	Water collected from the river or stream which runs towards the north
Louhing Nahkpa Pungphaitol Nahkpa	Many small grasses named Louhing Yampa, Pungphaitol (*Eleresine acgytiaca*)
Sida Natpa	A medicinal plant named Sida Hidak
Natang Nakhay	A kind of shrub
Napu Nasel Napee Singpee,	Some grass
Chtrai Loutrai,	A kind of plant
Yenpang Phaipangpa,	A kind of plant
Songlel Chingmathi Yaona,	Including Songlel Chingmathi plant
Yoymayaipu Santengkhiye.[5]	King Yoymayai was given bath.

These aforesaid different varieties of grasses, shrubs and plants were put to the water collected from different streams and rivers. At the time of the King's coronation ceremony of the Meitei king collected water was sprinkled by using grasses and plants while bathing.

The general theme of the above hymns give a detail description regarding the name of waters collected from different water bodies like streams and rivers. Apart of it, other essential plants and grass i.e. *sida nada natng, nakhai, napu nashel, napi shingbee, chatrei, loutrei, yenbng, phaibang,* are also mentioned. The water accumulated from different sites and articles and grasses were used to give bath to king before coronation.

It appears that the Meiteis were highly concerned about the water management. Since the rain is the source of the water-shed systems of Manipur, they developed sufficient devices to collect rain in time. Probably *Maiba Shanglen* (Department of priests) venerated wind to get rain as far as possible. When the kingdom was near facing impending drought due to absence of rainfall, Maharaja Chandrakirti, with the idea of solving such problem, he himself practically involved in '*Nong Kouba'* (Nong= rain and *Kouba* = call) by sailing in Hiyang (a big boat sailed only at the time of boat race.)[6] Besides, the Meiteis performed '*Nong Kouba*' ritual work by reciting hymns to please the rain god in the following varnacular manner:

Manipuri Version	*English Translation*
"Selthong Wukunong,	Rain blows from west direction
Teengna Leiphol Nong,	Heavy rainfall
Thongnang Takhel Khungam Nong,	Heavy rain comes from west direction
Arol Thangyai Nong,	Rain in horizontal shape
Khongchi Nathet Nong,	Rain can wash whole body
Ngalpa Nongchai Nong,	Rain comes from different directions
Thongnang Mayang Khungam Nong,	Rain blows from west
Kouna kounu Nong,	Rain from the north-west direction i.e.

Manipuri Version	*English Translation*
	Kouba Kounu peak of Kouru hill
Yeereng Yeekham Nong,	Rain takes place for a very long time
Koireng Khungam Nong,	Heavy rain can disturb to the Koireng tribe due to heavy rain, the Koireng people cannot do anything.
Tolem Tolngou Nong,	Rain blows from Tolem Tolngou direction
Nungsang Khongnang Nong,	Rain comes from the direction of Nungsang Khongnang
Taipong Tayang Khungam Nong,	Rain blows from the direction of Taipong Tayang
Selpee Kabow Khungam Nong,	Rain can disturb to the Selpee Kabow people due to excess rain, they can do nothing
Tharai Lemlei Nong,	Rain blows from the south direction
Pathok Puthok Nong,	Rain blows from Pathok Puthok or South direction
Lokha Haokha Nong,	Rain blows from the direction of Lokha Haokha
Haokha Chairel Khungam Nong,	Rain can disturb Haokha Chairel people
Selloi Langmai Nong,	Rain blows from Selloi Langmai direction i.e. Nongmaiching hill or east side
Langmai Nungkhong Nungnao Nong	Rain comes from Nungkhong Nungnao area of Nongmaiching hill - if cloud derives from Nungkhong Nungnao area, rainfall is possible in Manipur.
Yishingwo Chaoro	O! flooded
Wahi Manu,	A kind of insect - Saccharicoccus, saccharicola cockerell.
Koucheng Harou Chana,	Grasshopper also
Matingthekna Seengliye."[7]	Hustle huge and cry

The above hymns give detail names of various types of rain and rain cloud blows from different directions to Manipur. Rain god is requested to bring rain and to happen flood. The hymns also cite that the insects like *Wahi Manu*, grass hopper, etc. hustle loudly.

Before digging either canal or ponds, with the initiation of king an elaborate ritual work was done at the proposed site. They offered various articles including edible and unedible things to earth by delivering hymns. This ritual work was not only to please her but it was also an identical process of permission taken from her to dig canal or pond. The required birds, animal and articles for venerating the sites are following recorded as:

Manipuri Version	*English Translation*
Sareltee	Animal to be sacrificed,
Wokne	Pig
Khunu Ani	Two pigeon
Yen Ani	Two cock
Nganu Angoupa Ani	Two white duck
Leiremaki Mamangda Thawo	Put before goddess
Palthawo	Arrange a sitting place of a small single seated bench
Lathawo	Put banana leaf
Phithawo	Put clothe
Yot Phirak Ani	Two pieces of iron
Sel Ani	Two coins
Konyaiphu Ama Thawo	Put piece of one silver and gold
Leihul Taretlak Hulwo	Offer flowers seven times
Larupna Lalol Anilak Yaiwo	Put by overlapping two layers of banana leaves on upside-down position
Yura Halthok Halchil	Pured holy wine to two separate layers of banana leaves
Lalol Taret Taret Thawo	Put seven layers of banana leaves in two separate places
Hei Masing Malwo	Keep some fruits near the two sites where more two separate seven layers of banana leaves kept
Luklel Taret Sem	Arrange of seven special dishes
Laisolnapa Singkhara Khakwo	Reserve some firewood for reciting hymn
Meipa Chingduna Saphutphee Ama	By making fire, meat cooked at a pottery
Chapalphu Ama Thongkhatwo	Cooked rice at a pitcher

(Contd.)

Manipuri Version	*English Translation*
Satee Latol Amada Thatuna Laida Katwo	By putting cooked meat to a top piece of banana leaf offered to god
Yeerangpulta Yeesing Sokwo	Take water by using small pitcher,
Yura Haptuna, Halthokpana Yimmang Thangwo-Halchilpana Yimming Thangwo	At first poured the holy wine to the fore front site where the seven pieces of banana leaves were put by ivelapping for the second time, pured the holy wine to the back site (closer to body) where the seven pieces of banana leaves were put by overlapping.
Sing Ama mam Poituna	By holding one each fire wood,recite hymn,
Anima Lalnatuna Thamwo	Put two pieces of firewood by overlapping.

Before staring actual ritual work, the protected god or goddess of that site should be venerated first.

The hymns for this adoring are given below in varnacular language.

Manipuri Version	*English Translation*
Haya Tmpa Leimulol Taretmawo,	O! Creater,goddess of the seven layers of the earth.
Laihalol Taretmawo,	Makers of the seven different layers.
Thoupee Leiphanpee Nangna Selpee Kapo Pangna Leiphanbane,	Thoupee Leiphanpee makes south-eastern side of the earth.
Ngangoi Leirampee Nangna Thongnang Leirampane,	Ngangoi Leirampee creates western side of the earth.
Thoupee Leiphanpee Ngangoi Leirampee Nang Taipane.	Thoupee Leiphanpee and Ngangoi Leirampee were requested.
Tampak Leisung Leisoiyampeeyo, grasses,plants etc.	Goddess of upper layer and creater of
Huplaka, Haraya, Honteka Selpalka	The creater of grass, plant and animal
Poklipee Nangpu Taipane.	you are venerated.
Yongmuka Yongselka, Nuwokka Paipangka,	The creater of different animals like black-monkey, monkey, wild pig
Kheiroika Wupengka,	(Paipang is nick name of pig), squirrel, Wupeng,
Tengsitka, Naosangka,	Tensit, Naosang, Khuping and Khupai is worshipped to please.

Manipuri Version	English Translation
Khupingka Khupaika, *Poklipeewo Nangpu Taipane.* *Tara Katongnuka* *Wengmika* *Chakchaga* *Chahaoka* *Morsi Naoremtol Kalipee Nngpu Taipane.*	The creater of edible items like Tara Katongnu, Wengmi, Chakcha, Chahao (tasted black rice), Morshi (akind of paddy), is worshipped to please.
Leilol Leimaki Yaingchaipeewo.	Powerful creater of different layers.
Wupeeka Wurelka, Tlmuka *Tlhaoka Sohika Keehika,*	The maker of different trees like Wupee Wurel, Talmu,
Poklipee Nngpu Taipane.	Talhao, Sahi and Kuhi is venerated to please.
Nasu Hepungthou Nsu *Hepemsingpu Chakcha* *Lalkupeewo* *Haipaki Taipane.*"[8]	You are prayed by your grand-sons and daughters for their prosperity.

The above hymns mention the female dieties makers of the seven different layers. It also gives the brief description of the duties of the dieties of seven layers. Goddess *Thaopee Laiphanpee* was assigned to make layer of east side whereas Ngangoi Leirampee was responsible to form layer of the west. Both of dieties were worshipped for their amicable duties. Diety like *Tampak Leisuk Leisoiyampee* (the maker of plant, animal and food grain) (All these things come to birth on her lap) was prayed for her exceptional duties. You are prayed to bestow welfare and prosperity on our human being.

Either public or kings' own ponds were not permissable to be used before inauguration. Usually the Meiteis believed that the use water of these ponds were uneasy one before inauguration. Thus, the Meiteis performed inaugural ritual ceremony by offering many edible and unedible things to diety who dwelt inside and outside the newly made pond by narrating hymns. Those things to be offered are given below:

Manipuri Version	*English Translation*
Phaklong	A kind of mat made of flat pieces of bamboo
Phamphi Ama	One seat of god's clothe
Phirak Ani	Two pieces of clothe
Yot Ani	Two pieces of iron
Sel Ani	Two coins
Phi Ama	One clothe
Konyai Asengpa Ama	A holy piece of a gold and a piece of silver
Chapi Laisan Nongta	A kind of metal
Sarel Ama	One sacrificial animal
Nganu Ama	One duck
Khunu	Pigeon
Yel	Hen
Saphutphu Ama	One pitcher for cooking meat
Manungta Mathak Mathum Maroi Suna Hapwo	Keep or mix all required spices
Yeerengpul Ama	One pitcher for taking water
Kampee Taret	Seven earthen vessel
Leiri Taret	A kind of seven white flower
Lapot Taret	Seven bundles of banana leaves
Singpot Taret	Seven bundles of firewood
Khangkha Pot Taret	Seven basket used for keeping edible things
Khamen Pot Taret	Seven baskets of brinjal
Pal pot Taret	Seven baskets of arum
Uchek Marum Taret	Seven eggs of birds
Yerum Taret	Seven eggs of hen
Hei-Lei	Fruit-flower
Pana-Kwa	Betel leave and betel nut
Leisang Khekwaiba	A kind of beautiful flower
Lei Ayampa	Many flowers
Laphoi Lawu	Bunch of banana
Thara Pana Ama	A bunch of fruit
Hei Manam Naipa Ama	One sour fruit
Pana Phaipok Ama	A twin betal leaf
Kwa Phaibok Ama	A twin betal nut

(Contd.)

Manipuri Version	*English Translation*
Likol Maril Phattaba Ama	One cowrie which is not properly opened
Asi Kheipik Yaona	Include all these
Latha Potthafee stipulated site	Display all the required things to a
Kom Mahakpu	Tank itself
Wutangna Khara Sawo	To a convenient site of the pond, Khara a kind of bamboo net made of knitting Wutang bamboo pieces to keep all the required offering things
Mayai Ani Halwo	Make a hole at the centre of khara net
Atuta	That
Nongta	A kind of metal
Laism	Hair of an animal
Likol Maril Phattapa Hullo	Cowrie which is not properly opened was put or throw
Wuchiwa Achouba Amata	To a bamboo contained full of leaves at its top
Matolta Phiral Angouba Ama Yetwo	Keep a white flag at the top of bamboo
Lng Mapalna Teelpa Langsung Asangpa Ama	A long small rope thread made of combination by nine different threads
Pungou Ama	A light red clothe or pinkish
Watolta Kiwo	Tie at the tope of bamboo
Laset Lalot Taret Thatuna	Being put seven layers of banana leaf pieces
La Longna Thawo	Put banana leave upside down
Cheng-Yerum	Rice-egg
Pana Phaibok	Twin betal leaf
Kwa Phaibok	Twin betal nut
Laphoi Laphang Chang Thokpa	Banana set of chang pair number
Hei Manam Naipa	Sour fruit
Leisang Khekwaipa	A beautiful flower
Khayom Yomtuna	Being tied together on a half of banana leaf by keeping fruits and rice
Pathom Taret Pulwo	Seven piece of bamboo to be tied

Manipuri Version	*English Translation*
Watolta Langsung Asangba Atuka Pulwo	Tied to the top of bamboo by using a long small thread of rope made by the combination of different thread
Leipakta Sangna Thawo	Put in a long position to the surface of bank
Kom Mayaita Wuchiwa Achouba Yungwo	Erect a bamboo containing full of banana leaves at its top portion of the centre of pond or hole
Cheng-Yerum,Hei-Lei,Pana-Kwa Leisang Yaowo	Include rice-egg,fruit-flower, betal leaf-betal nut, green flower
Yerumti Machin Thukaituna	Make a hole at the top of egg
Konyai Ama	A gold piece and a silver piece
Lang Tharei Mapop Manga	Five buds of Eupatorium birmanicum should be kept at the hole of egg
Khayom Lakchilwo	Start to perform the rite of Khayom.

Before starting actual ritual work, the protected god or goddess of that site should be venerated first.

The hymns recited at the time of inauguration are mentioned below in vernacular language:

Manipuri Version	*English Translation*
"Tampak Leimulolwo Leihaorolwo	Apok Chanu Apok Chanu, the goddess of layer was named
Khumwoi Yangwai peewo Leihaorolwo,	differently as Tampak Leimulolwo,
Tampak Leisuk Leisoi Yampeewo Leisuk Leisoi	Khamwai Yangwaipeewo and Tampak Yampiwo
Tampak Thepee Tingthou Hupla Charaka Poklipuyo	The upper layer that grasses,herbs and other plants grow
Konteka	Area protected by upper layer goddess
Salpalka Paklipeewo	O! creater of field
Tampak Leimurol Leihaorol	Both upper and inner layers
Malem Tampak Leimathak	On the lap of the earth
Asita Apokpa Asalpa	Everything like plants and animals reside on this earth
Aku Ayelpawo,	Earth provides all the things
Pukhari Turel Achoupaki Mapu • Woipa Nangna	You owner of pond and big river came to emerge Phaokhtlapaki, on this being world

(Contd.)

Manipuri Version	*English Translation*
Nasu Heputhou Hepem masingna Ngasi Korou Numitmata,	Today, your grand sons and daughters
Lalol Taret Ngeitheengyei	Arrange seven layers of banana leaves
Chengngou Phahapna	Offered good rice
Yerum Kangkhilna,	Being kept egg on rice
Heirang Thepcham Yeina,	Being kept properly all the fruits
Asi Koirou Numitta Ngaiwariye.	Today you are waited
Mayum Tampak Leirol Taret Matakisung Karakwo	You please climb up from the interior of seven layers of earth
Laicha Yeerol Taret Matakisung Karakwo.	You please move up from seven layers of water
Karou Nonglol Taret Matakisung Kumalkwo,	You please come down from the seven layers of the sky
Chakpee Laisng	Kind of flower
Nongtarik Kolthawo.	Keep a kind of thing
Korou Nonglupan Angoupa,	Pure white silver
Mallem Leisna Angangpana	Red clay
Paotakchapane	Inform to god
Heina solwo."[9]	Start to recite hymns.

The above hymns mention both upper and inner layers of the earth. *Apok Chanu* who is named differently as Khamwoi Yangwaipeewo, Tmpak Leisuk Leisoi Yampeewo, dwelt both layers (various grass and other plants grow on you upper layer and you are the owner of ponds and rivers.) All the grass, plants, ponds and river reside on you i.e. earth. All the people associated with you, would prepare some fruits, eggs, rice and seven layers of banana leaf. You please come out through seven layers of earth, though you reside inside the earth. Though you dwell under water, you please come up through seven layers of water. Though you live in the sky, you please come down through the seven layers of the sky. O god! associated with cloud, water and earth, is adored with due respect and love. Thus the hymns was recited to aforesaid words.

The Meitei kings developed a sufficient knowledge to safeguard those river and canal, banks and dikes. They believed that the collapse of those protective systems was due to irate of water gods like Wangpurel and others. So, they hatched out the devices to persuade those water gods and goddess. Usually, the Meitei kings carried out two forms of ritual works like sacrifice of animal and offering of edible and unedible articles and things with reading hymns to check untold incidents. During the reign of Maharaja Narasing at Khumidok, river dike was crumped. And it was repaired under the care of the kings by sacrificing white buffallo and edible and unedible things.[10] The essential things and hymns which are used not to break down those guarding systems are mentioned below in varnacular language.

Manipuri Version	*English Translation*
Yusingpul Ahanpa Amata,	To a new pitcher
Ayuk Ngalna Eeshing sokwo,	Take water in early morning
La Wupna Thawo,	Put banana leaf by upside down
Heiruk Hapo.	Keep pieces of fruit
Wuchimi Watol Aphapa Ama,	A good top portion of bamboo bearing full of leaves
Phiral Angoupa Ama Thawo,	Keep a white flag
Wataiyo,	Make compromise by narrating
Yeesing Pul Khilwo,	Keep water pitcher
Yimki Yimpeerelta Waitawo,	Hand over everything to the owner of that area to make compromise
Yimki Karaltsuna,	Yimki=of the house, Karalsuna=fire place; centre of place where worship was done
Yeesing sokpatee Ningsa Holkano.	Do not breathe when one takes water
Chithek Marita Wai Teiyo,	Rub with water to the floor of the four corner of worshipping area
Laphu Mari,	Four banana plant
Chu Mari,	Four sugarcane
Wuchiwa Mari,	Dwarf bamboo plant having full of bamboo leaves on upper portion
Phiral Mari Thetlo.	Keep four flags
Heiruk Mari Semtuna Thao	Put four dishes of fruits
Mayaita sollo."	Recite hymns at the centre of four corner.

(Contd.)

The hymns are recited on the following varnacular language:

Manipuri Version	*English Translation*
Chakmaring pawo, Tangmaringpa, Mungmaringpawo,	Four protector gods i.e. Chakmaringpa, Tangmaringpawo and Kento of four directions of the earth
Kentowo	
Nangkhoi Marimana	You - four
Leikhong Leirai Kairapatee	If the embankment has collapsed
Chetna Ngakwo.	(You) safeguard carefully
Yeemmangta Haipati Tumaringpa Tangmaringpa	Front bank of river is guarded by god Yimningta Tumaharapa Back embankment is guarded by god
Tumaharapa	
Nangti Nongseet Nonghum Chetna Ngakwo,	You do protect carefully the powerful blowing win
Thongpullel Leichilpul cheepunglol,	Having got combination with wind, water started to pierce the river bank
Nongpok Leitonghuk	Break down east or front bank of riv^r due to bore by water
Tonghukpa	Pierce
Leipakki Yampha Phachilwo.	Tie and fill up the clay of river bank
Maipok Maipahalpa	Creater of the Earth god -represents Sanamahi
Leika Lengpa,	He is further to expand the creation of earth
Tongwo Asum Solwo	.Tongwo=live, Asum Solwo=Thus recite hymns
Nanaipu Apha Nungaipa Kuperamwo.[11]	Requested to bestow prosperity for your servant.

The above hymns mentioned clearly about the four proginators of the *Chakpas* i.e. *Chkmaringpawo, Tangmaring pawo, Mungmaringpawo* and *Kentowo*. Please you do protect the impending disturbances on the bank of river and canal. Tumaringpa and Tumaharapa were assigned to control the wind blows from front and back respectively. The head priest also should act to reconcilate with god. God was requested to bring the welfare and prosperity. In such way hymns were recited.

During the reign of Ura Laichingkhu, the chief of Moirang, the entire people of the principality requested to the chief to carry out *Nong Kouba* (call rain). Complying the request of his subjects, he (chief) called upon all the singers, priests and other people. Thus, Moirang chief with his subjects performed the *Nong-Kouba* ritual with hymns being read. These hymns are given to the following varnacular language.

Manipuri version	*English Translation*
"Eyum Thanjing koirel Nongwo	Rain blows from Thangjing hill to south-west direction.
Khoukhu Nonghou Nong-wo,	Rain likely to fall heavily
Shalthong Wakku Nong-wo, *south-west direction*	Rain comes from Shalthong i.e. from Nungkhong Nungnao Nong-wo, Rain comes from east
Chairel Suktu Nong-wo,	Rain comes from Chairel i.e. South of Moirang
Shelloi Langmai Nong-wo,	Rain blows from Shelloi Langmai side
Hirei Lairei Nong-wo."[12]	Rain supplied by Hirei Lairei goddess.

The hymns simply tell about the name of rain and rain clouds blows from different directions.

Usually, the Meiteis performed ritual work at the fishing '*shoy*' (wier site to catch various fishes abundantly). Those articles which are needed to offer fishing *shoy* area are given below in varnacular language:

Manipuri version	*English Translation*
"Moibung Maril Hodabna Luning Huk *shape*	Cunch which is not opened its mouth should be tied to the hind of cone-fishing trap made of bamboo pieces.
Sha Maya Manba Likkon Ngakha oi,	Being replaced Ngakha fish-Green bark, Puntius Phutunis by cowrie seems to be the teeth of animal
Malem Leisna Angangpana Sharengsha,	Being made Shareng fish-Wallago attu- of red clay

(Contd.)

Korou Longlupan Angoubna Nganoy oi,	Being made Nganoy fish-Barbus Sarana Caudimarginatus by pure white silver
Choinou Sana Sel masungnaibana	Gold bowl which is marked of long spots was used to take fish and thus Shcy
Nga Kotlaga Shoy Honge,"[13]	(weir) inauguration ceremony was held.

The offering of the aforesaid articles to the fishing *shoy* or wier was simply to catch plenty of fishes.

REFERENCES

1. Leishemlon (MS), p. 51.
2. Irom Amubi Singh(transcribe); *Nunglon,* Imphal, 1981, p.6, and also *Leihou Naophamlon,* 1980, pp. 5-6.
3. Pakhangba Nawonba (MS), pp. 3-4.
4. Phambalol (MS), p. 5.
5. Ch.Hemchandra Singh (transliterate), *Numit Kappa*, 2008, Imphal,p.31.
6. L. Ibungohal and N. Khelchandra Singh (ed), *Cheitharol Kumbaba,* 1968, p. 317.
7. Chanam Hemchandra (transliterate), *Lairol Thounirol*, Imphal, 2004, p. 63.
8. *Ibid.*, pp. 33-34.
9. *Ibid,* pp. 12-14.
10. L. Ibungohal and N. Khelchandra Singh, *op. cit.*, p. 267.
11. Chanam Hemchandra, *op. cit,* pp. 37-39.
12. Chanam Hemchandra (transliterate), Keke Kangleirol, Imphal, p.12.
13. Moirangthem Chandra Singh (transcribe), Panthoibi Khongkul, Imphal, 1972, p. 20.

Note: Translation work of Hymns done with the help of Ch. Hemchandra Khaba.

6

Conclusion

By and large, the prestine Meiteis systematically developed a response to the monsoonal climatic regime of the kingdom of Manipur and always were prepared to mould its' topographical structure. They got experience through different social and natural phenomena since the dawn of neolithic till the modern time. According to topographical variation, they definitely engaged in different occupations. On the other hand, the rulers in order to achieve their political aim, carried out public welfare related works and secondary traits like construction of dikes, fishing *shoy* (fishing wire), canals, moats, repairing river beds, dredging rivers, ponds and fishing canals etc. Manifestly, the early Meitei State experienced two types of despotisms like hydrodespotism and agrodespotism. The peculiar feature of hydrodespotism is the management of non-productive water works whereas agrodespotism emerges when king controls irrigated canals. The Asiatic Meitei villages had specific characteristics.

(1) They erected dikes across the streams.
(2) They dig the village communities' own irrigated canals.
(3) Different individuals created their separate smaller irrigated canals.
(4) They were very familar with rainfall farming.

However, the rainfall regime and topography were important reasons to determine the mode of the occupation of the Meiteis. Monsoon rain provided enough water for field agriculture and the villagers themselves manipulate the necessary landscape either to collect rain water or to bring the water of streams to the cultivable fields. The natural situation kept the king out of the general scene. Therefore, he was not in position to get involved in any programme of field water management for cultivation. Though water was so needed to wet rice traditional Meitei agriculturists, probably it would not set up any connection between the irrigated water management and statecraft since the commencement of neolithic settlement in the valley till the first half of 18th century. But the Meitei kings between this aforementioned long span of period actively invested their energy to engage in a large number of non-productive water controlling projects relating to public welfare schemes. Under such a circumstances the Meiteis are always ready to act as dynamic device to govern the State successfully. Both the Meitei kings and the general people controlled the natural water for their own benefit. They also manipulated related landscape according to their convenience. The King managed water as a part of his public welfare schemes and led to draw maximum loyalty from his subject while the people handled water for the successful cultivation which enabled them to pay taxes timely to the State. In this stage, hydrodespotism came to exist .

Marx states that irrigation is an instrumental factor for the centralisation of administrative apparatus (State apparatus) to co-ordinate and develop large-scale hydraulic works. Despotism and the ruling bureaucracy are reasonable for such type of public work. He also believes that irrigation work prevailed on the first form of Asiatic society.[1] His idea of irrigation is well advanced and it applies to some specific society. He further thinks that if such type of organisation once existed, a hydraulic economy characterised by division of labour, intensive cultivation and co-operation on a large scale and the State took the part of managerial role played by ruling bureaucracy.[2] Large scale government-managed irrigation work is the source of oriental agriculture resulting in Oriental Despotism. It is highly centralized State. As a matter of fact, "oriental State controlled the strategic means of production and most importantly the cultivable land." No doubt, hydraulic economy is synonimous with oriented society. Though it has many characteristics, only three elements are considered as most important. "Hydraulic agriculture involves a specific type of division of labour. It intensifies cultivation. And it necessiates cooperation on large scale."[3] Thus, irrigated cultivation demands more labour, systematic organization and effective management. Obiousely, it is the method implied by the king to achieve a systematic social control. Such enterprise would be one of the vital technique applied by the king to promote statecraft. Incidentally, all these characteristics and many more are observable in Manipuri socio-political and economic infrastructure since the past many centuries. Hydraulic power-play and social control are intrinsic to Manipuri society.

Some scholars successfully adhere to the Marxian idea of irrigation and its managerial power despotism. They , however, plead that both irrigation and despotism are the secondary traits.[4] Since irrigation is secondary trait, its work i.e. water management work is an essential force to bring about a mature State. According to Mellion:

> "there is the implicit relation between irrigation and political processes leading to changes of social."[5]

Thus, irrigated water management always favours to create an atmosphere of centralization and a central tendency towards the development and maturation of a State..

It was during the kingship of Maharaja Garibaniwaz that a great transformation was took place in the spheres of socio-political conditions of the kingdom of Manipur. He was regarded as the greatest ever general of Manipur. During his period, territorial frontier of the kingdom extended from Ava in the east to Cachar in the west. In the south her influence reached as far as the water-shed flowing seawards and to the north her boundary extended for about nine days journey from the capital.[6] Apart his military valour, he posed himself to be an initiator of a new religion. Therefore, the king looked towards Hindu religion and he practically introduced it as a State religion. He, however, borrowed the idea of Hindu divine kingship. His idea of adoption of Hindu system of divine kingship was to make more people admire the king. The newly emerging trend brought to establish a virtual relationship between the dynasty of the Meitei kings and Arjuna, the great epic hero of *Mahabharata* which attributed a new decisive power and an ancient political legitimacy to power and prestige in the State. In addition to normal water work programme, he for the first time initiated to dig out a State-owned irrigated canal. This instance was the beginning of agro-managerial works under the care of the State. The coexistence of new Hindu divine right theory of kingship and a limited agro despotism came to prevail in the Meitei society. The question was how far Garibaniwaz was successful in drawing the loyalty of his subject by using a new divine kingship. It was not a successful attempt since a larger section of the entire population of the kingdom of Manipur had refused to embrace the new religion.

The natural topography of the kingdom of Manipur profoundly compelled the Meitei kings to care the water bodies in order to bring the welfare of the State. Technologically less developed Meiteis were attracted tremendousely to construct more water routes because of their presence around the water sheds including lake, marshes, swamps, streams and river. The availability of various water body systems would make the Meiteis easier to develop water transport.

It is believed that *pong* (raft) the earliest form of boat used by the Meiteis. It was made of two or three bunches of bamboo (sometimes it was made of banana plants) were used widely for river and canal transportation. Particularly, pole made of bamboo was served as oar to sail aforesaid type of boat. During the reign of king Khagemba, one Laiba Ungam Thaba used to sail his *pong* (raft) employing bamboo pole to Chengbi Leima canal. It is responsible task of the Meitei kings to undertake usual assignment of digging canals, dredging river beds and repairing river banks led to improve transport service. However, the invention of trunk boat or dug-cut canoes during the kingship of Meidingu Khuyoi Tompok would bring more convenient of river, canal and lake communication. Such type of transport mechanism definitely expertised to sail trans-lake regions and against the flow of river current with loaded or unloaded goods. Besides, it would help to promote fishing system and to bring a great improvement in trade and commerce.

The traditional Meitei villages were also found to reside along with the river and lake banks practically to get riverine and lake transport facilities and other advantageous. The plan settlement villages were highly influenced to specify even on their occupations. Thanga village was set up to the islet of Thanga located at the centre of Loktak lake. They engaged in fishing as their main occupation. Lake route was only the device to link up between the island village and outside places. Dug-cut canoes were only used in their daily transport. In the southern corner of the valley, villages like Wangu and Chiren were respectively installed on the bank of Manipur river. They used to trade their agricultural and handicraft products. The villagers of Chiren sailed their goods loaded big boat via Khodrak river, Loktak lake and Nambul river up to Khwairamband market to sell their home-made pottery products. Long rope made of bamboo piece was frequently employed to pull the big loaded boat, when the people sailed at upstream.

Obviously, lake and river served as the cheapest mode of transport resulted to come active an inter-village quick interaction. The changing trend intensified commercial activities of the villagers. Apart the transport and commercial purposes, the Meitei kings also paid more emphasis to handle river by installing dikes, deepening beds and repairing banks. Under the stalwat of Meitei king, dikes were constructed across the river with elaborate ritual works. Such type of dikes were made with the object of protecting impending flood. Another dike was created in alternate season like dry or winter season to crop up water for daily using. It is also usually raised, when the kingdom was trouble of the scarcity of water due to long absence of rain.

The historical events exemplify that the prestine Meitei kingdom would experienced of hydraulic pattern of society. In fact, before the reign of Garibaniwaz, there was no more historical and literary sources recorded State own irrigated canals. But only one irrigated canal at Yarou was mentioned in *Cheitharol Kumbaba* the royal chronicle. During the kingship of Nara Singh two irrigated canals near god Puthiba had been reported. Another irrigated canal named *Pheidailoukhong* (irrigating canal) was also mentioned at the time of Maharaja Chandrakirti. The available data prove that the Meitei kings were hardly involved in building large scale irrigated canals; but like their predecessor, these kings widely undertook non-productive hydraulic works as their usual routine. Even though, the agro-depotism prevailed in Meitei society since the reign of Garibaniwaz, it will be an overestimate to term Meitei Despotism as an Oriental Despotism in which the power of the ruler was supreme. Because such type of society came to exist when the State own irrigated canals were installed extensively and large scale irrigated cultivation was done. Usually such programmes were possible only in semi-arid regions where the annual rainfall is less, vast area of agricultural lands are available, big perenial rivers rise from snow-cap mountain runs etc.

Generally the traditional Meiteis considered water as the source base of culture, power and economic functions. The handling of non-producing State sponsoring water works would generate ruling power and authority. Probably the concept of dwelling important gods in the water bodies was reminded as a source of cultural symbol. In the later period, it was from second part of the18th century that the Meitei king Maharaj Garibaniwaz introduced a system to dig irrigational canals. Thus hydraulic agriculture at low scale was inaugurated in Meitei society. The rainfall farming culture better known as hydroagriculture was still dominating in Meitei society because the dominance of seasonal monsoon rain, absence of big perenial river rising from big snow caped mountains, large areas of swamp and marshes and absence of good bottom land agricultural fields. The practice of hydraulic agricultural enterprise justified the king to have control over production and labour organizations. The proper utilization of water resources by making irrigated canals would give a great opportunity to the ruling elite to extract some portion of surplus production produced by the peasant cultivators. Thus, water was systematically evaluated with ritual works to be utilized in the sphere of culture and economic way of life.

It can be concluded that the existence and development of the Meitei civilization is highly concerned with the embodyment of water shed system in the kingdom. Therefore, Meitei kings initiated to launch various water work enterprises and performed practically different forms of ritual works relating to water bodies in order to strengthen their grip over his subject.

In the beginning chapter, the watershed systems like rivers, canals and lakes and the possibilities of controlling these water points were thoroughly considered. Further the climate and landscape favoured the hydraulic culture or hydraulic agriculture. The people inhabiting during the prehistoric time, the spread of their habitation to different areas, the migration of various ethnic groups to Manipur from the east and the west and their migration routes, the tales and the literary sources and the different statements made by a number of scholars are studied seriously for the simple fact that having a good historical past is sine quo non for a good society to emerge with a tradition of its own.

In the preceding chapter, wider understanding of water points controlling water body systems handled by the clan chiefs, the emergence of Kangla, the long history of supervising different water shed cared by the Meitei kings are clearly mentioned. A part of it, owning of fishing shoys or fishing wiers by the clan chiefs and Meitei kings are separately highlighted. Basic features of Asiatic mode of production is also discussed. The management pattern and manipulation of landscape by the king and common people are put separately so as to present a serious study of the working of hydraulic power play in the Meitei society.

The history of rice culture and its ecological reflections, the changing development systems of cultivation i.e. Jhuming, permanent wet cultivation and transplantation, social formation, pattern of labour organization are put together. The water management typologies of the Meiteis of Manipur, Funans of Combodia, Ahoms of Assam and Tais of Thailand are separately studied.Incidentally we devote ourselves to study about the relation between the culture and water shed points in Manipuri history.

REFERENCES

1. Bottomore (ed), A *Dictionary of Marxist Thought,* England, p. 33.
2. Ronald Cohen and E.R.Service, *Origin of the State, The Anthropology of Political Evolution*, 1978, Pheladelphia, p. 70.
3. Karl A. Nittfogel, *Oriental Despotism, A Comparative Study of Total Power*, New Haven: Yale University Press, First Published 1957, pp. 3 and 22.
4. Henri J.M. Claessen, *Peter Skalnik, The Early State,* New York, 1979, p.9.
5. R. Cohen and E.R. Service, *op. cit.,* p. 72.
6. R. Brown, *Statistical Account of Manipur* (Rpnt), New Delhi, 2001, p. 60.

Bibliography

In English

Arambam, Saroj Nalini 2005, *The Court Chronicle of the Kings of Manipur*, Paratt Routledge Tylor and Francis Group, London and New York.

Bottomore, T.B. 1975, *Sociology a Guide to Problems and Literature*, New Delhi, Blakei & Sons.

Bottomore, Tom, *A Dictionary of Marxist.*

Brown, R. 1975, *Statistical Account of Manipur* (Reprint), Delhi.

Chandra, Bipan, *Karl Marx.*

Claesson, Henri J.M. and 1974, *Early State*, New York. Pater Skalnik

Cohen, R. and E.R. Service 1978, *Origins of the State: The Anthropology of Political Evolution*, Philadelphia.

Hodson, T.C. 1947, *The Meeteis.*

Houtart, F. and G. Lemercineir 1984, *The Great Asiatic Religions and their Social Formation*, New Delhi.

Kabui, Gangmumei 1991, *History of Manipur*, Vol.I Pre-Colonial Period, New Delhi, National Publishing House.

Manihar, Ch. (Tr.) 1983, *Naothingkhong Phambal Kaba*, Imphal

Manners, R.A. and 1975, *Theory in Anthropology, A Source Book*, David Kaplan Chicago, Aldine Publishing Co.

McMulloch, Major W. 1959, *An Account of the Valley of Manaipore*, Calcutta.

Morgan, Lewis Henery 1986, *Ancient Society*, New Delhi.

Service, E.R. 1975, *Origin of the State and Civilization:the Process of Cultural Evolution*, New York, Norton.

Sharma, B. Kullachandra 1987, *Ancient Principal Tribes of Manipur with Special Reference to Plain Tribes*, Seminar on Ancient History of Manipur, Imphal.

Singh, Heisnam Nilkant 2006, *Early Political System of Manipur and Thailand*, Imphal.

Singh, O. Kumar 1983, *Archaeology of Manipur*.

Singh, W. Ibohal 1986, *The History of Manipur* (An Early Period), Imphal, Manipur Commercial Co.

Thapar, Romila 1984, *From Lineage to State*, Bombay, Oxford University Press.

Venice to John Wilmot, 1829, *The Encyclopaedia Americana*, Interest Lonal Edition, New York, Americana Corporation.

Wittfogel, Karl A. 1957, *Oriental Despotism, A Comparative Study of Total Power*, New Haven, Yale University Press.

In Manipuri

Bhogeshor, Oinam (Transcribed) 1984, *Toreirol Lambuba*, Manipur State Kala Akadami.

Bhogeshor, Oinam 1967, *Ningthourol Sheireng*.

Bhogeshor, Oinam 1983, *Moirang Ningthourol Lambuba*, Imphal.

Chandra, Moirangthem 1967, *Gambhir Singh Nonggaba* Poknapham Singh Publication, Imphal.

Chandra, Moirangthem 1972, *Panthoibi Khangkul*, Manipur Sahitya Parishad, Singh Imphal.

Hemchandra, Chanam 1996, *Kangleirol* (An Account of different places of Manipur with important historical event) Imphal.

Ibungohal, Lairenmayum 1967, *Cheitharol Kumbaba*, Imphal. Singh & Ningthoukhongjam Khelchandra Singh (Trd.)

Khelchandra, Amubi, N. 1994, *Sagei Shalairol*, Meiteigi Yek *Salai Yumdaba Puya* O. Bhogeshor,N.Ibochouba State Kala Akadami, Imphal.

Luwang, Angou (ed.), 1983, *Pakhangba Nongkarol*, Imphal.

Moirangthem Manaoyaima Chengleiron, Manipur Sahitya Parishad, Imphal. Singh (Transcribed) 1979.

Nilabir, Sairem 2007, *Laining Nat Amashung Puwarigi Mityengda Kala* (reproduced), Imphal.

Phajabi, Hijam Chanu (Tr.) 2005, *Kangla Nunglon Laiphamlen*, Imphal.

Singh, M.Gourachandra 2004, *The Manipur Topology* (A treats of place, name in Meitei).

Singh, N. Ibochouba 1982, *Thiren Mairam Leeba*, Imphal.

Singh, N. Manaoyaima 1986, *Tutenglon,* Kakching.

Singh, R.K. Sanahal 1985, *Pangal Thorakpa,* Imphal.

Articles

Chandra, Bipan, *Karl Marx His Theories of Asian and Colonial Rule, Centre for Historical Studies*, School of Social.

Science, Jawaharlal Nehru University, New Delhi.

Nodiachand, M. 1985, *Moirang Salai*, an article presented to S.R. Institute sponsored Seminar on History of Manipur before 1500 A.D.

PLATES

Pulling boat to the river bank

A man sailing raft (*Pong*)

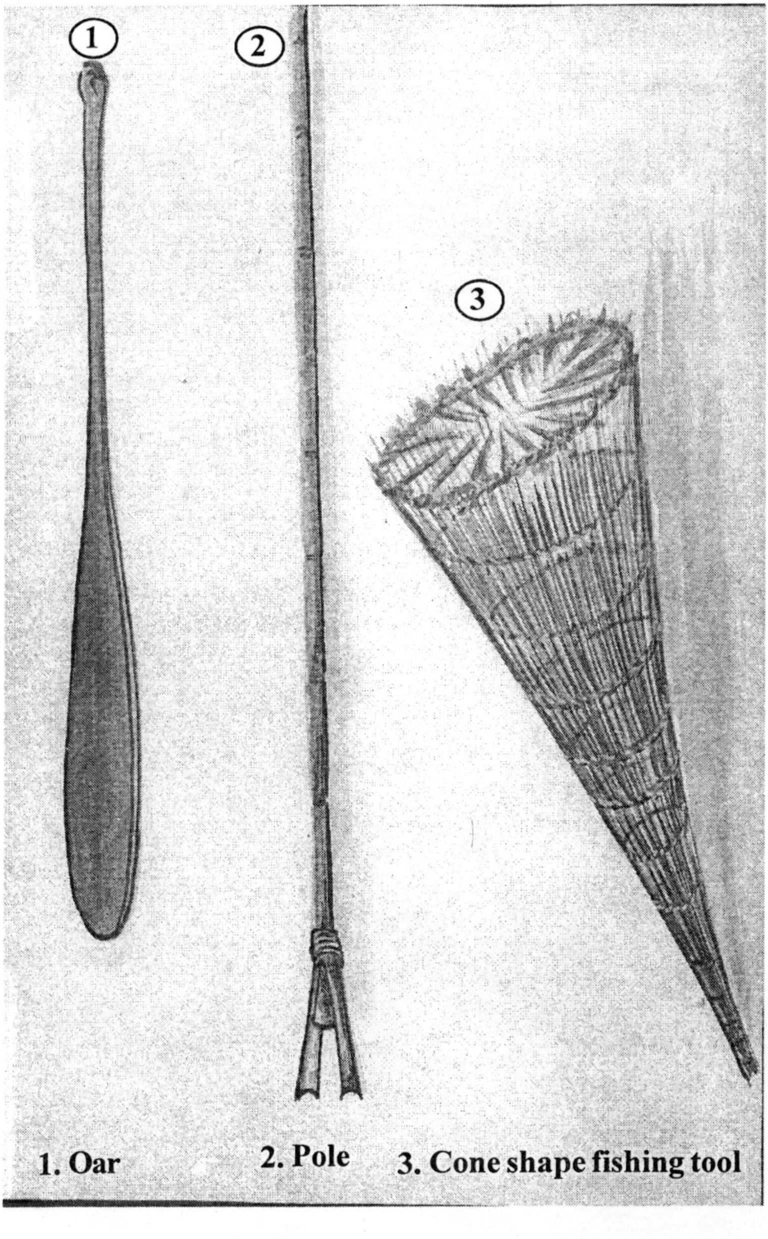

1. Oar 2. Pole 3. Cone shape fishing tool

Sailing boat on the river

Akum Shoy (Weir)

Sailing loaded boat in trans-lake region

Aka *Shoy* (Weir)

Index

S

❑❑❑